Getting Fit With Food

101 healthy eating recipes

Shana Lee Conradt

Happy & Healthy Cooking

Shana

To place an order: www.getfitwithfood.com

ISBN: 978-0-615-37381-2

Edited by Maria L. Turner
Photographs by Shana Lee Conradt

Printed in the United States of America
    by Print Source Plus of Appleton, Wisconsin (www.printsourceplus.com)

Athenos® is a registered trademark of Kraft Foods (www.kraftfoods.com)
BUSH'S® is a registered trademark of Bush Brothers & Company (www.bushbeans.com)
FASTSIGNS®-Appleton is a registered trademark of FASTSIGNS (www.fastsigns.com/267)

Acknowledgments

Graham, I love you. I thank God that we are partners in building this beautiful life.

To my hero, my mentor, my teacher, my strength – to you dad: You taught me more through your eyes than with your words. You remind me to treasure every breath my lungs take. Your faith is unwavering. In your aggressively encouraging way, you continually help me push past the point of comfort in everything I do.

To the kindest woman I've ever known – to you mom: Your patience is immeasurable. Your love is unending. You teach with serenity, gentleness and thoughtfulness. You are like no other. Thank you for standing by me, for typing for me and for tasting all my recipes.

Because of you, my parents, I realize there are no limitations to this gift we call life. I cannot express how I love you both.

A special thank you to the following:
- Maria, my editor, business partner, sound board and my friend (I couldn't have done this without you!)
- Lee and Andy for an amazing camera and for your love
- Jay and Susan for a gorgeous kitchen, great friendship and guidance
- Nancy for taking the time to care about me as a businesswoman and for introducing me to Doug
- Doug for believing in me and confidently introducing me to Marshall
- Marshall for thinking I was crazy and being OK with it
- Athenos, Bush Brothers & Company and FASTSIGNS

Finally, thank you, Lisa, for being a part of my growth and for being beside me for so many years.

Table of Contents

How to Get Fit With Food

I'm not really a cook. I am a health-conscious woman who didn't want to eat boring food, so I learned how to cook.

I married the most amazing man who believes in my endless list of dreams. Together, we created two beautiful boys who we have the honor of parenting and loving.

Aside from pregnancy, my weight has remained unchanged since high school. I do love green vegetables; however, I do not eat the cliché health foods, like rice cakes or tuna, very often.

When I co-founded Ellipse Fitness in 2002, I vowed to teach clients that healthy food could be enjoyed *without sacrificing taste*; I promised not to recommend rice cakes, spinach and plain chicken breast *for every meal* and I still guaranteed their *weight loss success*.

That's the philosophy I've carried throughout this cookbook. Here, you'll find healthy recipes that are not your typical "diet food." My hope is you'll find that not only can healthy eating be delicious, but it also can be fun!

So, before you dive into the fun, let's first touch upon a few basics.

Preservatives

There are a number of factors that come into play when selecting one brand of food over another. The first thing you should ask yourself is, "How close to 'natural' is this food?"

If you weigh 150 today and 149 tomorrow morning, where did the pound go? Seriously… where?

Well, some of it had to leave you. Yep, that's right: You "got rid of it." Bodily functions and the level at which they are being carried out is crucial in weight loss.

In very simple terms, think of preservatives as obstacles. When we eat natural, minimally processed foods low in preservatives and rich in fiber, vitamins and minerals, our bodies use what they need and then liberate the waste. Not only do preservatives hang out longer, they actually hinder

the natural excretion process by getting in the way of waste attempting to leave the body in a timely manner.

If you cut back on preservatives and select more natural/organic foods, your digestive system will be able to function at an optimal level, and you will be more likely to achieve your weight loss/healthy lifestyle goals.

Carb Labels

Ingredient lists are made in order of how much of that item is in the product, meaning you'll find the largest amount of the initial ingredient in the food. A great rule of thumb is that the first three ingredients on a label should be natural, unaltered, clearly recognized and easily pronounced. For example, 100% whole wheat flour and enriched wheat flour are two very different things; stone ground whole wheat and unbleached wheat flour are not the same; and sprouted grains and enriched unbleached flour are completely different worlds. When selecting a carbohydrate, use this rule often. Veer toward 100% whole wheat, organic and preservative-free grains, breads, pastas, crackers and cereals.

Carb Basics

The American Diabetic Food Exchange List states that one carbohydrate exchange is 15 grams. For a smaller person, one exchange will be sufficient for main meals. For a larger individual, a man or someone who trains intensely, that

can be bumped up to two exchanges for breakfast, lunch and supper. Examples of one exchange of carbohydrates are:

- ½ cup cooked pasta
- 1 slice bread
- ⅓ cup cooked rice
- 2 ounces cooked sweet potato
- 3 ounces baked potato

When it comes to crackers or cereals, check the ingredient list first and then use the label information to determine how much your serving size will be.

Serving Sizes

Keep in mind that the serving size on a label is determined based on an average guess. According to how we sometimes assume a serving size works, a 100-pound woman, a 200-

pound man and a 6-year-old should be eating the same amount of cottage cheese.

Really? I don't think so!

Use the label information to calculate how much of that particular food you are going to eat or how much fat and protein a serving size has. However, realize you are not average and that average serving size isn't meant for you.

Which Protein to Eat

One protein exchange is 7 grams of protein. The amount of fat in the exchange determines if it is a very lean, lean, medium fat or high fat exchange. The American Dietetic Association defines a very lean protein exchange as having 35 calories and 1 gram of fat. Examples of very lean exchanges are:

- 1 ounce turkey or chicken breast
- 1 ounce white fish fillet
- 1 ounce canned tuna in water
- 1 ounce shellfish
- ¾ cup nonfat cottage cheese
- 2 egg whites
- ¼ cup egg substitute
- 1 ounce fat-free cheese

These would be considered very "clean" choices and should be eaten whenever feasible.

Typically, a lean exchange will have 2 to 3 grams of fat and is also a good choice. If the fat content of an ounce (or more specifically an exchange, which is 7 grams of protein) is more than 3 grams, it is probably not a good choice and should be avoided.

To determine the fat content, take the grams of protein listed for a serving size and divide it by 7 (one exchange) to determine the total exchanges the serving is. Then, multiply that number by 3 (the maximum amount of fat that you should have per exchange for it to still be a good food choice). If the fat content is less than that number, you can eat it!

When it comes to processed meats, such as lunch meats, hot dogs and sausages/brats, it is a bit tricky. Lean lunch meats will have more preservatives, so for 7 grams of protein, you will need more than an ounce of meat.

For this reason and because preservatives are such a hindrance, try to avoid lunch meats when possible and go for a more natural meat option. Hot dogs, although fat-free at times, have too many additives and preservatives to ever be a good choice. Brats and sausages, especially organic brands, will meet the above criteria occasionally and are becoming more and more available!

Eggs

Organic eggs are recommended for a number of reasons. Free-range birds are allowed more space to roam and are therefore cleaner, laying eggs that are less likely to carry salmonella. They are typically fed a superior diet, which is evident in the thicker, smoother texture of the shell, as well and the richer yolk color and firmer appearance of the white.

The look and taste of organic eggs is healthier and more desirable.

Low-Carb

It is rare for me to suggest low-carb foods because typically that means that preservatives and additives have been increased to lower the carbohydrates. It also usually means that fiber has been removed from the product.

As a result of these alterations, shelf life – and more importantly, nutritional values – decrease as well.

That said, there are a few instances where the lower-carb options are favorable. Light flat breads can be found that have 100% whole wheat flours as the main ingredient and are as low as 15 grams of carbohydrates per serving. There are also lower carb tortilla/wrap options that have fantastic, natural ingredients.

Check out a few labels and determine if the foods you are considering are right for you.

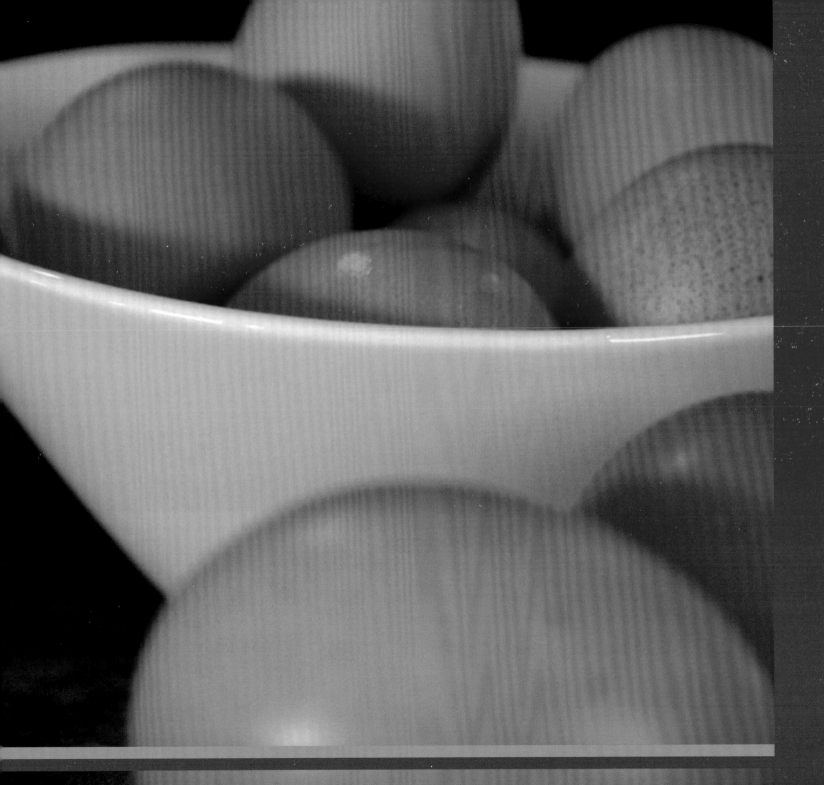

Breakfast Bagel Sandwich

Prep time: Less than 5 minutes
Cook time: 5 minutes

Ingredients

1 piece light string cheese

½ c. liquid egg whites

Salt and pepper

Cayenne pepper

Parsley

Nonstick cooking spray

2 slices turkey

Bagel thin

1. Shred a piece of light string cheese and set aside.

2. Whisk together egg whites and seasonings.

3. Spray nonstick pan with cooking spray, pour in eggs and cook over medium heat with cover on. Do not flip.

4. Fold egg into quarters and place on top of bagel thin.

5. Top with turkey and shredded cheese.

6. Place open-faced breakfast sandwich under broiler until top is toasted and cheese is slightly browned.

*Serves 1
Calories: 200
Fat: 4.5g
Carbohydrates: 24.8g
Protein: 33g*

Eggs & Potatoes O'Brien Skillet

Prep time: Less than 5 minutes
Cook time: 5 minutes

Ingredients

Nonstick cooking spray

½ c. mushrooms

1 c. potatoes O'Brien

Pinch red pepper flakes

1 t. olive oil

Salt and pepper

1 clove garlic

1 t. fresh rosemary

1 c. liquid egg whites

1 T. salsa

1. Prepare ingredients: Slice mushrooms, press garlic and chop rosemary. Set ingredients aside individually.

2. Spray nonstick pan with cooking spray.

3. Sauté mushrooms, potatoes, red pepper flakes, olive oil, salt and pepper over medium heat for 7 to 10 minutes.

4. Add rosemary and garlic and cook an additional 3 minutes.

5. Pour in egg whites and cook until fluffy.

6. Top with salsa.

Serves 1
Calories: 277.5
Fat: 2.5g
Carbohydrates: 31.6g
Protein: 28.6g

French Toast & Scrambled Eggs

Prep time: Less than 5 minutes
Cook time: 5 minutes

Ingredients
Nonstick cooking spray
¾ c. liquid egg whites
2 slices raisin bread
¼ t. cinnamon
¼ t. thyme
Seasoning salt
Salt and pepper

1. Spray nonstick pan with cooking spray and place over medium heat.

2. Pour ¼ cup egg whites into bowl big enough for bread to fit within.

3. Dip bread slices in egg whites quickly on both sides and place in pan.

4. Sprinkle French toast with cinnamon and flip to cook on second side when first side is browned to liking.

5. Whisk together egg whites with thyme, seasoning salt, and salt and pepper to taste while second side of French toast cooks.

6. Remove French toast from pan; set aside momentarily.

7. Spray pan again, add seasoned egg whites and scramble eggs.

Serves 1
Calories: 232.3
Fat: 2.5g
Carbohydrates: 25.5g
Protein: 24.9g

Egg & Turkey Breakfast Wrap

Prep time: Less than 5 minutes
Cook time: 5 minutes

Ingredients

Nonstick cooking spray

½ c. liquid egg whites

Salt and pepper

¼ t. fresh thyme

1 oz. sliced turkey

1 T. low-fat shredded
   mozzarella cheese

Low-carb whole wheat wrap

Serves 1
Calories: 107.5
Fat: 4.3g
Carbohydrates: 16.2g
Protein: 25.8g

1. Spray nonstick pan with cooking spray and place over medium heat.

2. Whisk egg whites with salt, pepper and thyme.

3. Pour egg white mixture in heated pan, cover and cook until set.

4. Slide eggs onto wrap, top with turkey and cheese, and roll up.

Spinach-Mushroom-Feta Frittata

Prep time: Less than 15 minutes
Cook time: 45 to 50 minutes

Ingredients

3 oz. dry pasta (2 c. prepared)
Nonstick cooking spray
1/3 c. red onion
2 cloves garlic
8 oz. sliced mushrooms
Salt and pepper
5 c. liquid egg whites
3 oz. ATHENOS nonfat feta cheese
1½ c. fresh spinach
1 t. thyme
Aluminum foil

Serves 6
Calories: 172 • Fat: 2.3g
Carbohydrates: 12.3g • Protein: 21.8g

1. Preheat oven to 350 degrees.

2. Cook pasta, rinse in cold water and set aside.

3. Dice red onion and press garlic cloves.

4. Spray nonstick pan with cooking spray, place over medium heat and sauté the red onion, garlic and mushroom with salt and pepper for 5 minutes. Remove from heat and set aside in bowl to cool.

5. Stir together egg whites, cooked pasta, crumbled feta, spinach, sautéed vegetables and thyme in large bowl to create frittata mixture.

6. Spray 9" x 13" baking pan with nonstick cooking spray and add frittata mixture.

7. Cover with aluminum foil and bake 20 minutes. Uncover and bake 25 to 30 minutes more until center is set.

Chicken Sausage Frittata

Prep time: 10 to 15 minutes
Cook time: 30 to 45 minutes

Ingredients

1.5 oz. dry pasta (1 c. prepared)

½ c. broccoli florets

½ c. cauliflower florets

½ c. carrots

Nonstick cooking spray

6 oz. cooked chicken or
   turkey sausage (lean meat)

⅓ c. onion

4 c. liquid egg whites

1 oz. ATHENOS nonfat feta cheese

1 t. fresh thyme

Salt and pepper

1 oz. Pecorino Romano cheese

1. Preheat oven to 350 degrees.
2. Cook pasta, rinse in cold water and set aside.
3. Prepare ingredients: Chop broccoli, cauliflower and carrots; slice sausage into ¼" pieces and dice onion and thyme. Set each aside individually

Serves 4
Calories: 228.2
Fat: 3.3g
Carbohydrates: 16.4g
Protein: 30.2g

4. Spray nonstick pan with cooking spray, place over medium heat and cook sausage, broccoli, cauliflower, carrots and onion for 5 to 7 minutes. Set aside to cool.
5. Stir together egg whites, cooked pasta, vegetables, onion-sausage mixture, crumbled feta, thyme, salt and pepper in large bowl to create frittata mixture.
6. Spray 9" square glass baking pan with nonstick cooking spray, add frittata mixture and top with Pecorino Romano cheese.
8. Bake uncovered in oven for 30 to 45 minutes or until the center of the frittata is set.

Andouille Sausage & Cheese Omelet

Prep time: 5 minutes
Cook time: 15 minutes

Ingredients

1 Andouille chicken sausage

2 T. diced onion

1 clove garlic

Nonstick cooking spray

½ c. liquid egg substitute

Salt and pepper

¼ t. fresh thyme

1 piece light string cheese

1. Dice chicken sausage and onion and press garlic clove.

2. Spray nonstick pan with cooking spray, place over medium heat and sauté the sausage, onion and garlic for 5 to 7 minutes. Remove from heat and set aside in bowl to cool.

3. Whisk together eggs, thyme, salt and pepper.

4. Spray skillet with cooking spray again, pour in egg mixture and cook over medium heat with cover on for 5 minutes. Do not flip.

5. Shred string cheese.

6. Pour sautéed sausage-onion-garlic mixture over half of the omelet, sprinkle with shredded cheese, fold other half of omelet over top and cook another 3 minutes until cheese is melted.

Serves 1
Calories: 180
Fat: 3.2g
Carbohydrates: 3.5g
Protein: 31.3g

Mushroom Egg Cups

Prep time: 5 minutes
Cook time: 30 minutes

Ingredients

Nonstick cooking spray

2 c. liquid egg substitute

1½ c. fresh mushrooms

1 T. fresh chives

¼ c. green onions

⅓ c. shredded reduced-fat sharp cheddar cheese

Salt and pepper

Serves 3
Calories: 108
Fat: 1g
Carbohydrates: 2g
Protein: 20g

1. Preheat oven to 350 degrees.

2. Spray standard 12-muffin tin with nonstick cooking spray and fill each muffin well with ⅓ cup egg substitute.

3. Chop mushrooms, chives and green onions, and divide equally into muffin wells.

4. Sprinkle shredded cheddar cheese equally into each muffin well.

5. Season with salt and pepper to taste.

6. Bake uncovered for 30 minutes.

Breakfast Burrito

Prep time: 5 minutes
Cook time: 5 minutes

Ingredients

2 T. green pepper

2 T. red pepper

2 T. onion

1 to 2 T. Serrano chili

1 t. garlic

1/8 t. fresh oregano

1 T. fresh cilantro

1 c. liquid egg substitute

Salt and pepper

2 low-carb corn tortillas

2 T. fresh salsa

4 T. BUSH'S® Refried Beans – Fat Free

2 oz. reduced fat Mexican cheese

1. Prepare ingredients: Dice green and red peppers and onion; remove seeds and ribs from chili pepper and dice; and chop garlic, oregano and cilantro. Set each aside individually.

2. Whisk together eggs, red, green and chili peppers, onion, garlic, oregano, cilantro, salt and pepper.

3. Spray nonstick pan with cooking spray, pour in half of the egg mixture, cover and cook over medium heat until set (about 5 minutes).

4. Lay egg onto tortilla.

5. Spread 2 tablespoons refried beans over egg, top with half of the cheese and salsa and then fold into burrito.

6. Repeat steps 3 through 5 for second serving.

Serves 2
Calories: 162
Fat: 3g
Carbohydrates: 16g
Protein: 22g

Shana says...

The egg white makes up most of an egg's weight. It consists almost completely of water. Egg whites are very low in calories. They have a trace amount of fat, which is usually regarded as negligible. There is no cholesterol in egg whites, and within the white's water are 40 kinds of protein.

The white of an egg is also much less likely to carry salmonella than yolks are.

Egg whites, therefore, are an excellent source of very lean protein.

Egg whites (or egg substitutes) are also quite versatile in culinary use. Consider these options:

- Use in combination with vegetables, meats and seasonings to make awesome omelets.
- Mix with seasonings, rice, pasta, vegetables or almost any other leftovers in frittatas.
- Throw together a crust (or buy one) and leave out the pasta or rice, and you've got a wonderful quiche.
- Cook them, adding tomatoes and a slice of light cheese, for a great egg sandwich.
- Mash hard-boiled egg whites, blend with your choice of seasonings, zero-calorie mustard and maybe a touch of Athenos nonfat Greek yogurt and you have yourself an egg salad that won't quit!

Healthy, tasty, endless options: They're not just for breakfast anymore!

Banana-Berry-Pecan Pancakes

Prep time: 5 minutes
Cook time: 10 minutes

Ingredients

⅓ c. fat-free cottage cheese

⅓ c. ATHENOS nonfat Greek yogurt

2 pkgs. whole grain cranberry oatmeal

2 bananas (⅓ c. sliced)

8 egg whites (or 2 c. liquid egg whites)

¼ c. chopped pecans

Nonstick cooking spray

Berries or light syrup

1. Combine all ingredients in food processor to create pancake batter.

2. Spray small to medium nonstick pan with cooking spray, pour in one-third of pancake batter to cover skillet bottom and sprinkle with pecans.

3. Cover and cook until pancake is set (approximately 2 minutes), flip and cook 1 minute more.

4. Remove from pan and top with berries or light syrup.

5. Repeat steps 2 through 4 for remaining two servings.

Serves 3
Calories: 259
Fat: 10g
Carbohydrates: 25g
Protein: 24g

Jazzed-Up Meatballs

Prep time: 15 minutes
Cook time: 30 minutes

Meatball Ingredients

1¼ lbs. ground venison

1¼ lbs. extra lean ground turkey

½ c. fat-free ricotta cheese

⅓ c. panko bread crumbs

¼ c. onion

2 T. Anaheim chili

2 T. flat-leaf parsley

½ oz. grated Pecorino Romano cheese

3 to 4 cloves garlic

¾ T. fresh thyme

½ t. ground oregano

1 large egg

2 t. herb salt

Ground black pepper

Nonstick cooking spray

Shana says...

Quaint little shops featuring uniquely seasoned olive oils, specialty vinegars and a variety of flavored salts and peppers are popping up all over the place. These distinctive items will add new zest, tang, essence and aroma, allowing you to put your own personal touch on any recipe you chose to try!

Serves 10
Calories: 231.1
Fat: 7.5g
Carbohydrates: 9g
Protein: 30.8g

1. Prepare ingredients: Dice onion and chili, press garlic, chop parsley and thyme, and beat egg. Set each aside individually.

2. Combine all ingredients in large bowl to create meatball mixture.

3. Form into ping-pong ball-sized meatballs.

4. Spray nonstick pan with cooking spray, place over medium heat and cook meatballs, rolling to brown all sides evenly. Set aside to cool.

Sauce Ingredients

3 c. plain jarred marinara sauce

Pinch crushed red pepper finely chopped

1 T. fresh chopped parsley

¼ c. minced onion

1 T. steak sauce

3 dashes Worcestershire sauce

2 dashes hot sauce

1 t. herb salt

1. Chop crushed red pepper and parsley and mince onion.

2. Combine all sauce ingredients in same pan in which meatballs were browned.

3. Let sauce simmer gently while covered for 15 minutes.

4. Return meatballs to sauce and simmer another 5 minutes.

Deviled Eggs

Prep time: 10 minutes
Cook time: 10 minutes

Ingredients

7 eggs

1 green onion

1 stalk celery

1 finely chopped egg white

½ c. ATHENOS nonfat Greek yogurt

1 T. Dijon mustard

1 t. prepared horseradish

1 T. fresh chopped parsley

½ T. fresh dill

Paprika

1. Hard-boil eggs, run under cold water and let soak several minutes to cool.

2. Peel off eggshells, cut eggs in half and discard yolks.

3. Mince green onion and celery and finely dice two of the egg white halves (leaving 12 halves to be filled).

4. Combine all remaining ingredients, excluding paprika, with onion, celery and diced egg whites.

5. Fill 12 egg white halves with creamy mixture.

6. Sprinkle with paprika.

Serves 6
Calories: 47
Fat: 0g
Carbohydrates: 1g
Protein: 12.5g

Steak Bites With Spicy Sauce

Prep time: Less than 5 minutes
Cook time: 10 to 15 minutes

Ingredients

½ T. olive oil

1 clove garlic

1 shallot

Salt and pepper

1 lb. top sirloin

2 c. tomato sauce

¼ t. cayenne pepper

¼ t. celery salt

1 to 1½ T. horseradish

2 to 4 dashes Louisiana hot sauce

2 dashes Worcestershire sauce

1 T. steak sauce

¼ to ½ t. crushed red pepper flakes

1 oz. vodka (optional)

Serves 6 (with ¼ c. vodka sauce)
Calories: 192
Fat: 7g
Carbohydrates: 5g
Protein: 24g

1. Swirl oil in skillet and place over medium heat.

2. Mince garlic and shallot, add to skillet, along with salt and pepper to taste, and sauté for 2 minutes.

3. Cube sirloin, add to skillet and brown to desired wellness.

4. Remove cooked sirloin from pan, leaving behind garlic and shallot.

5. Create dipping sauce by adding tomato sauce and remaining ingredients to skillet and simmer over low heat for 5 minutes. For an alcohol-free option, leave out the vodka. For more or less kick, adjust amounts of hot sauce and red pepper flakes according to taste.

Mini Chicken Sausage & Onion Puffs

Prep time: 30 to 40 minutes
Cook time: 15 to 20 minutes

Ingredients

3 cloves garlic

1 red onion

Nonstick cooking spray

1 pkg. crescent roll dough

1 c. ATHEN🌐S nonfat Greek yogurt

1 ½ T. dry ranch seasoning

7 chicken sausages

1 t. olive oil

Salt and pepper

1. Preheat oven to 350 degrees.
2. Chop garlic into moderate-sized chunks and slice red onion into strips.
3. Spray nonstick pan with cooking spray, add garlic and onion, and sauté for a few minutes until onion becomes soft. Remove from heat and set aside to cool.
4. Roll out crescent roll dough and cut in half. Place half in refrigerator.
5. Cut remaining half of dough into 24 equal squares and press each square until thin and flat.
6. Combine yogurt and ranch seasoning and place ¼ t. mixture on each dough square.
7. Slice each chicken sausage into 7 equal pieces.
8. Place 1 chunk garlic, 1 strip onion and 1 slice chicken sausage on top of yogurt.
9. Bring corners of dough squares to center and press together.
10. Dip index finger into olive oil and rub very small amount onto uncooked dough puffs and season with salt and pepper to taste.
11. Remove refrigerated dough and repeat process from steps 4 on.
12. Bake puffs for approximately 10 minutes until dough turns golden brown.

Serves 6
Calories: 218
Fat: 5g
Carbohydrates: 21g
Protein: 24.5g

Just Getting Started

Feta Burgers With Greek Yogurt

Prep time: 10 minutes
Cook time: 10 minutes

Ingredients

1 lb. ground round

4 oz. ATH€N@S nonfat feta cheese

1 clove garlic

2 T. shallot

¼ t. cumin

¼ t. cayenne

½ c. ATH€N@S nonfat Greek yogurt

1 T. green onion (no white)

1 t. chives

½ t. lemon juice

10 pieces fresh spinach

Salt and cracked pepper

1. Mince garlic, shallot, green onion and chives individually and set each aside.

Serves 10
Calories: 124
Fat: 5.8g
Carbohydrates: 5g
Protein: 16.7g

2. Combine ground round, feta, garlic, shallot, cumin and cayenne in large bowl.

3. Form meat mixture into 1½" mini burger patties, season with salt and pepper to taste and brown in skillet over medium heat.

4. Remove burgers from heat when desired wellness is achieved and place on serving platter.

5. Whisk together yogurt, onion, chives and lemon juice in bowl.

6. Top burgers with piece of rolled spinach.

7. Place dollop of yogurt mixture on top of spinach and secure with toothpick.

8. Sprinkle with salt, cracked black pepper and chives.

Creamy Crabby Spinach Dip

Prep time: 10 minutes
Cook time: 20 minutes

Ingredients

1 clove garlic

$^1/_3$ c. onion

¼ c. fresh parsley

½ c. ATHENOS nonfat Greek yogurt

½ c. fat-free cottage cheese

8½ oz. all-white crab meat (squeezed and drained)

1 t. lemon juice

1 t. Worcestershire sauce

¾ t. lemon-and-herb seafood seasoning

$^1/_8$ t. white pepper

Salt and pepper

$^1/_8$ c. grated parmesan cheese

5 oz. frozen chopped spinach (thawed, squeezed and drained)

*Serves 4
Calories: 112
Fat: 2g
Carbohydrates: 9g
Protein: 17g*

1. Preheat oven to 350 degrees.

2. Chop garlic, onion and parsley leaves coarsely and add to food processor.

3. Add ¼ cup yogurt and cottage cheese into food processor with other ingredients and blend until almost smooth.

4. Combine crab meat, yogurt mixture, lemon juice, Worcestershire sauce and seasonings in large bowl.

5. Fold in chopped spinach.

6. Spread dip mixture into 9" square baking dish and sprinkle with parmesan cheese, salt and paper.

7. Bake 20 minutes or until bubbly and remove from oven.

8. Stir in remaining ¼ cup yogurt and sprinkle with lemon-and-herb seasoning.

Boneless Buffalo Tenders With Dip

Prep time: 10 minutes
Cook time: 10 minutes

Ingredients

1 c. Louisiana hot sauce

1 T. honey

14 oz. chicken breast

Nonstick cooking spray

2 oz. ATHENOS nonfat feta cheese

½ c. ATHENOS nonfat Greek yogurt

1 clove garlic

1 T. parsley

1 T. chives

1 T. green onion

½ t. lemon juice

1 T. onion

Salt and pepper

Serves 5
Calories: 127.6
Fat: 2.7g
Carbohydrates: 1.1g
Protein: 23.7g

1. Whisk together Louisiana sauce and honey in a bowl.
2. Slice chicken into 1" x 2" strips.
3. Place chicken strips into sauce to marinate. (Refrigerate chicken and sauce for increased heat.)
4. Spray skillet with nonstick cooking spray and cook chicken over medium heat until tender (about 10 minutes).

Feta-Yogurt Dip

1. Prepare ingredients: Crumble feta cheese, press garlic, chop parsley, chives, green onion and onion. Set each aside individually.
2. Stir together feta, yogurt, garlic, parsley, chives, green onion, lemon juice, onion, salt and pepper.

Roasted Red Pepper Dip

Prep time: 5 minutes
Cook time: No cooking required

Ingredients

16-oz. can BUSH'S® **BUSH'S** BEST
    Great Northern Beans

1 fire-roasted red pepper
    (jarred, in water)

2 oz. ATHENOS nonfat
    feta cheese

1 c. fat-free cottage cheese

½ t. cumin

1 clove garlic

Salt and pepper

1. Drain and rinse beans.

2. Combine all ingredients in food processor and process until smooth, dip consistency.

3. Chill for at least an hour for maximum flavor.

Serves 6
Calories: 121
Fat: 2g
Carbohydrates: 15g
Protein: 12g

Creamy Bean Dip

Prep time: 5 minutes
Cook time: No cooking required

Ingredients

½ c. BUSH'S® Refried Beans – Fat Free

1 c. ATHENOS nonfat Greek yogurt

1 chipotle pepper in adobo sauce

½ c. tomatoes

¼ c. green onions

½ c. BUSH'S® Black Beans **BUSH'S**

Serves 3
Calories: 96
Fat: 0.5g
Carbohydrates: 11.5g
Protein: 13g

1. Blend refried beans, yogurt and chipotle pepper in food processor until smooth. Spread mixture in a layer at the bottom of a bowl.

2. Dice tomatoes and green onions.

3. Drain and rinse black beans.

4. Layer black beans, tomatoes and onions on top of dip mixture.

5. Stir everything together just before serving.

Shana says...

Like it muchos caliente? Leave in the seeds! An easy way to cut back on a bit of heat when cooking with peppers is to discard the seeds and the white ribs that run down the inside center of the pepper. Although the majority of the heat is in the inner wall of the pepper, the seeds and ribs carry heat, too!

Just Getting Started

Avocado Taco Dip

Prep time: 10 minutes
Cook time: No cooking required

Ingredients

¼ c. BUSH'S® Black Beans
1½ c. BUSH'S® Refried Beans – Fat Free
⅓ c. taco sauce
1 c. ATHENOS nonfat Greek yogurt
1½ T. taco seasoning
1 c. salsa
2½ c. salad greens
1 c. tomatoes
½ c. green onions
½ avocado

1. Drain and rinse black beans.

2. Blend black beans, refried beans and taco sauce in food processor until smooth and spread in thin layer over platter.

3. Whisk together yogurt and taco seasoning and spread over bean layer.

4. Shred salad greens and dice tomatoes, green onions and avocado.

5. Layer salsa, lettuce, tomatoes, onions and avocado over taco-seasoned yogurt.

6. Chill for at least an hour before serving.

Variation: Add cooked ground turkey or chicken for a spin!

Serves 6
Calories: 148
Fat: 2.7g
Carbohydrates: 22.8g
Protein: 11g

Just Getting Started

Super-Dooper Salads

Shrimp & Chicken Fiesta Salad

Prep time: 15 minutes
Cook time: 15 minutes

Ingredients

Nonstick cooking spray

16 oz. chicken breast

Salt and pepper

16 oz. frozen shrimp

16-oz. can BUSH'S® Garbanzo Beans

16-oz. can wild rice

15-oz. can diced seasoned tomatoes

15-oz. can corn

15-oz. can BUSH'S® Black Beans

16-oz. can BUSH'S® Pinto Beans

4-oz. can diced green chilies

2 c. bell pepper (any color)

Juice of 1 lime

2 T. fresh cilantro

Serves 8
Calories: 262
Fat: 2.4g
Carbohydrates: 35.5g
Protein: 26.5g

1. Spray skillet with nonstick cooking spray and cook chicken thoroughly over medium heat (approximately 15 minutes).

2. Remove chicken from heat to cool, season with salt and pepper, and dice.

3. Rinse shrimp with cool water until thawed and allow to drain.

4. Drain and rinse beans, drain rice, tomatoes and corn, chop pepper and mix all in large salad bowl with chicken and shrimp.

5. Stir in lime juice and season with salt, pepper and chopped cilantro.

Summer Chicken Salad

Prep time: 15 minutes
Cook time: 15 minutes

Ingredients

4.75 oz. dry pasta (3 c. prepared)

2 13-oz. cans chicken breast in water

5 stalks celery

Red bell pepper

Yellow bell pepper

½ medium red onion

½ T. fresh rosemary

½ T. fresh thyme

1 c. ATHENOS nonfat Greek yogurt

⅓ c. spicy no-calorie spicy mustard

1 T. dry ranch seasoning

Salt and pepper

Serves 8
Calories: 200
Fat: 6.1g
Carbohydrates: 14.6g
Protein: 22g

---

1. Cook pasta, rinse in cold water and set aside.

2. Drain canned chicken.

3. Chop celery, peppers and red onion and place in bowl with drained chicken and pasta.

4. Chop rosemary and thyme, whisk together with yogurt, mustard, ranch seasoning, salt and pepper, and fold into ingredients in bowl.

5. Chill salad for at least an hour before serving.

Tortellini Salad

Prep time: 20 to 25 minutes
Cook time: 15 minutes

Ingredients

20 oz. cheese tortellini

1 clove garlic

4 T. sliced olives

½ red onion

½ English cucumber

1 c. grape tomatoes

1 T. olive oil

Salt and pepper

3 T. capers

4 oz. ATHEN⊙S nonfat feta cheese

½ c. ATHEN⊙S nonfat Greek yogurt

1 t. lemon zest

1 t. fresh thyme

1. Cook tortellini according to package directions, rinse in cold water and set aside.

2. Mince garlic clove, slice olives, chop red onion and cucumber, and cut grape tomatoes in half. Set each aside.

3. Add olive oil to nonstick pan, place over medium heat and add garlic.

4. Add tortellini, season with salt and pepper to taste, and cook pasta until lightly browned

5. Add vegetables, olives and capers and cook an additional 2 minutes.

6. Remove from heat, let cool slightly and then combine skillet ingredients with feta cheese and yogurt in salad bowl.

7. Garnish with lemon zest and thyme.

Serves 8
Calories: 272
Fat: 9.5g
Carbohydrates: 32.4g
Protein: 16.5g

Steak & Grilled Veggie Salad

Prep time: 5 minutes
Cook time: 10 to 15 minutes

Ingredients

8 oz. round steak

1/8 t. white pepper

1/8 t. black pepper

1/4 t. salt

1/8 t. celery salt

1/8 t. dry minced onion

Pinch finely crushed red pepper

1/2 T. olive oil

3 asparagus spears

1/4 c. strips red onion

8 grape tomatoes

Salt and pepper

Fresh spinach

Romaine lettuce

1 T. balsamic vinegar

1 t. Dijon mustard

1/2 t. red wine vinegar

1 oz. ATHENOS nonfat feta cheese

1. Cut steak into strips.

2. Combine dry seasonings and sprinkle over top side of steak strips.

3. Warm olive oil in skillet over medium heat, add steak strips seasoned side-down, cook for 2 minutes, flip and cook 2 more minutes.

4. Remove steak strips from pan, leaving liquid behind in pan.

5. Cut asparagus spears and tomatoes in half and red onion into strips.

6. Reheat pan until liquid warms, add vegetables, salt and pepper, and sauté for 5 minutes.

7. Place steak and veggies on a bed of mixed spinach and romaine lettuce.

8. Whisk together balsamic vinegar, mustard and red wine, and drizzle over steak, followed by crumbled feta.

Serves 3
Calories: 180.2
Fat: 9g
Carbohydrates: 4.4g
Protein: 20g

Super-Dooper Salads

Cucumber & Cranberry Salad

Prep time: 5 minutes
Cook time: No cooking required

Ingredients

1 c. sliced cucumbers

¼ c. red onion

1 tomato

1.5 oz. ATHEN⊕S
     nonfat feta cheese

¼ c. dried cranberries

Salt and pepper

1. Slice cucumbers, dice red onions and remove seeds from tomatoes and chop into pieces.

2. Combine veggies in salad bowl, toss with crumbled feta and dried cranberries.

3. Season with salt and pepper to taste.

Serves 2
Calories: 121 • Fat: 3.3g
Carbohydrates: 18.4g • Protein: 5.8g

Super-Dooper Salads

Mexican Chicken Salad

Prep time: 15 minutes
Cook time: 10 to 15 minutes

Ingredients

Nonstick cooking spray

1 lb. chicken breast

$1/_3$ c. onion

1 clove garlic

11-oz. can corn

21-oz. can BUSH'S® Black Bean  Fiesta Grillin' Beans®

15-oz. can Spanish rice

Salad greens

1 c. reduced-fat shredded sharp cheddar cheese

1. Spray nonstick pan with cooking spray and cook chicken thoroughly over medium heat, adding water, if necessary.

Serves 6
Calories: 280
Fat: 3g
Carbohydrates: 34g
Protein: 28g

---

2. Remove chicken from pan, let cool and dice.

3. Mince onion and garlic and sauté in sprayed pan over medium heat until onion softens.

4. Add chicken back into pan with onion, garlic, corn, beans and rice. Cook until heated through.

5. Top salad greens with heated chicken mixture and sprinkle with cheese.

Fresh Fruit Salad

Prep time: 5 minutes
Cook time: No cooking required

Ingredients

4 c. fresh fruit
melon
mangoes
grapes
blueberries
¼ T. lime zest
1 T. fresh lime juice
1 T. fresh mint

1. Cut melon and mangoes into bite-sized chunks and place in salad bowl with grapes and blueberries.

2. Zest lime with cheese grater and add zest to fruit.

3. Add lime juice and toss salad.

4. Chop mint and sprinkle to garnish salad.

Serves 4
Calories: 72.5
Fat: 0g
Carbohydrates: 18.2g
Protein: 1g

Eight-Layer Salad

Prep time: Less than 5 minutes
Cook time: 35 minutes

Ingredients

3 eggs

2 c. romaine lettuce

3 c. cucumbers

2 c. tomatoes

1 c. peas

6 oz. Canadian bacon

Nonstick cooking spray

½ c. ATHENOS nonfat Greek yogurt

¾ T. dry ranch seasoning

1 T. chicken broth

Salt and pepper

2 pieces light string cheese

Serves 4
Calories: 170
Fat: 5g
Carbohydrates: 11.6g
Protein: 22g

1. Hard-boil eggs, run under cold water and let soak several minutes to cool.
2. Shred romaine lettuce and arrange in bottom of tall salad bowl.
3. Dice cucumbers and tomatoes and add each in its own layer on romaine.
4. Add a layer of peas.
5. Dice Canadian bacon into bite-sized pieces.
6. Spray nonstick pan with cooking spray, place over medium heat and fry bacon until browed. Let bacon cool and layer over peas.
7. Whisk together yogurt, ranch seasoning and broth and spoon over bacon layer. Season with salt and pepper.
8. Grate 2 pieces string cheese and sprinkle over yogurt layer.
9. Peel hard-boiled eggs, discard yolks, chop egg whites and place over cheese layer.
10. Chill for 4 hours and then stir layers together just before serving.

Broccoli & Cauliflower Salad

Prep time: 10 minutes
Cook time: 20 minutes

Ingredients

1 head broccoli

1 head cauliflower

2 c. carrots

6 oz. extra lean turkey bacon

1 oz. cashews

¼ c. sunflower seeds

½ c. ATHENⓈS nonfat Greek yogurt

2 T. light mayonnaise

2 T. no-calorie sweetener

1½ T. reduced-fat grated parmesan cheese

Salt and pepper

1. Chop broccoli and cauliflower (florets only), carrots, turkey bacon and cashews into bite-sized pieces.

2. Combine chopped veggies, nuts and sunflower seeds in large salad bowl.

3. Whisk together yogurt, mayo, no-calorie sweetener, parmesan, salt and pepper to create dressing and fold into ingredients already in bowl.

4. Chill at least an hour before serving.

Serves 6
Calories: 165
Fat: 8g
Carbohydrates: 13.5g
Protein: 13.5g

Shana says...

I hate the reputation salads have!

They don't taste good…. Only skinny people eat them…. If you want to be thin, you have to eat them.

You know what?

More of the salads found on restaurant menus are bad for you than the number that are actually good for you! Add-ons like cheese, dressing, nuts, tortilla chips and deep-fried chicken take away from the beautiful vegetables that should compose a healthy and tasty salad. And, these add-ons increase the calorie counts so much that a lot of salads have become almost equivalent in calories to those contained in a greasy burger. I often say that if you have to drench your salad in ranch dressing, you need to find a new vegetable!

Find vegetables that you enjoy the taste of and take a moment to appreciate the honest flavor of a salad. Or, enjoy the recipes that are in this chapter.

Either way, bring your salads back to the basics and back to the healthy option they should be!

Spinach Salad

Prep time: 5 minutes
Cook time: 10 minutes

Ingredients

6 oz. turkey bacon

4 c. fresh spinach

1 c. bean sprouts

8 oz. water chestnuts

½ T. red onion

½ c. no-calorie sweetener

¼ c. catsup

1½ T. white vinegar

½ T. Worcestershire sauce

½ T. olive oil

2 T. water

1. Brown turkey bacon in nonstick skillet, remove from pan to let cool and chop into bite-sized pieces.

2. Slice water chestnuts and place in salad bowl with spinach, turkey bacon and drained bean sprouts.

3. Chop red onion and add to blender with no-calorie sweetener, catsup, vinegar, Worcestershire sauce, olive oil and water. Blend well to create dressing.

4. Pour dressing over salad just before serving.

Serves 2
Calories: 163.5
Fat: 5g
Carbohydrates: 14.7g
Protein: 21.7g

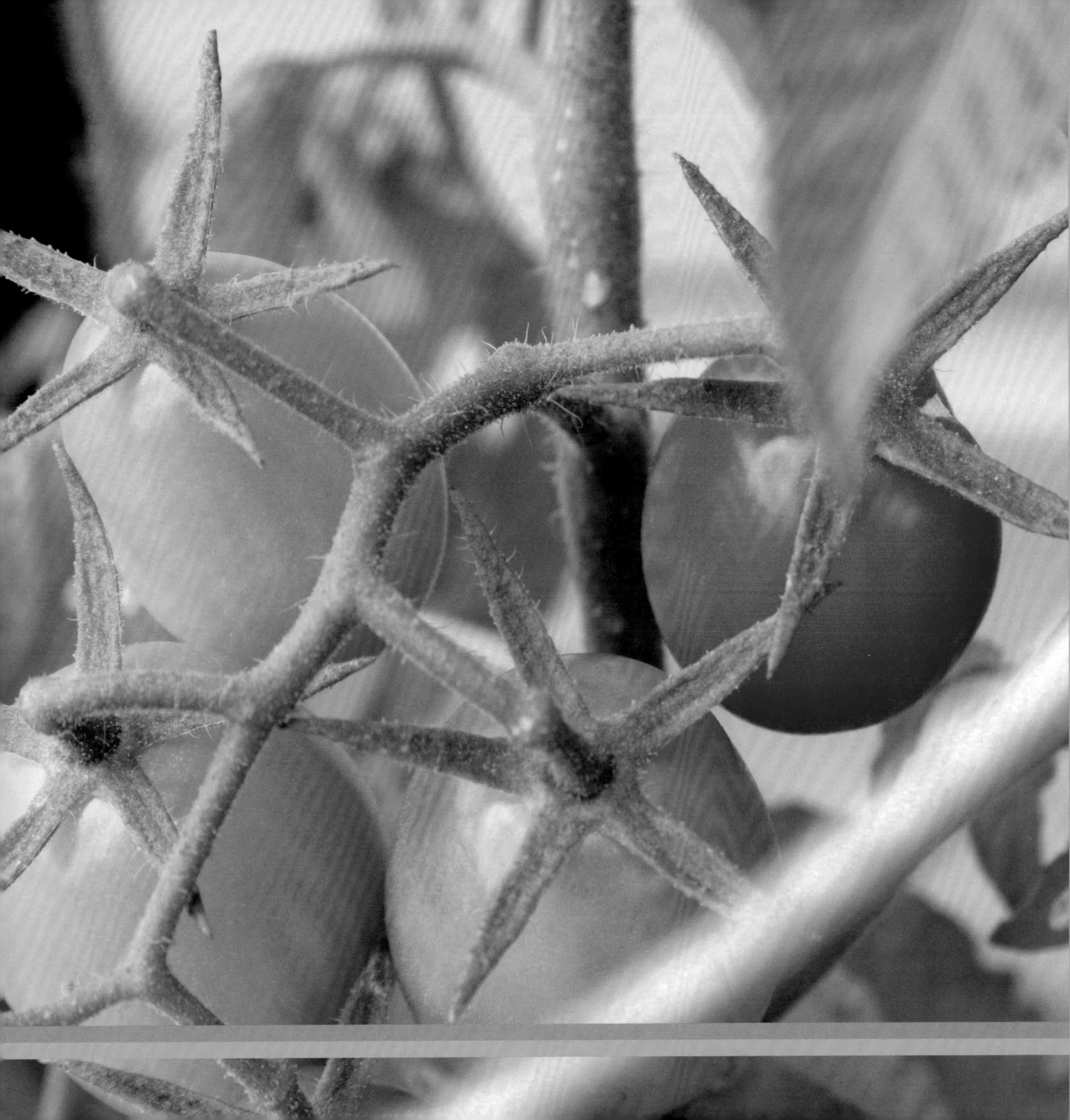

Earthy Options

Wild Rice & Ginger Stuffed Peppers

Prep time: 20 minutes
Cook time: 30 minutes

Ingredients

3 red bell peppers

⅓ c. green onion

1 c. cooked brown rice

1 c. cooked wild rice

Salt and pepper

¼ c. soy sauce

Pinch red pepper flakes

2 T. fresh squeezed orange juice

1 t. freshly grated ginger

1. Preheat oven to 350 degrees.

2. Cut off pepper tops and remove seeds and interior ribs.

3. Mix remaining ingredients together in a bowl.

4. Stuff each pepper with rice mixture, dividing evenly.

5. Place in baking pan and cook for 30 minutes, or until peppers are tender. Monitor cooking and if rice begins to get too brown, cover pan with foil and continue cooking.

Serves 3
Calories: 167.5
Fat: 0.4g
Carbohydrates: 31.5g
Protein: 4.7g

Chicken & Sundried Tomato Peppers

Prep time: 20 minutes
Cook time: 30 minutes

Ingredients

4 green bell peppers

⅓ c. onion

2 cloves garlic

1 oz. sundried tomatoes in water
(or rehydrate dried tomatoes)

½ c. baby bella mushrooms

1 medium sprig rosemary

1 lb. ground chicken breast

Salt and pepper

½ c. vegetable broth

1. Preheat oven to 350 degrees.

2. Cut off pepper tops and remove seeds and interior ribs.

3. Dice onion, press garlic cloves and chop tomatoes, mushrooms and rosemary. Set each aside individually.

Serves 4
Calories: 154.3
Fat: 1.6g
Carbohydrates: 6.8g
Protein: 27.3g

4. Brown chicken with onion, garlic, salt and pepper. Remove from heat and let cool slightly.

5. Combine chicken mixture with remaining ingredients.

6. Stuff each pepper with chicken-veggie mixture, dividing evenly.

7. Place in baking pan and cook for 30 minutes, or until peppers are tender. Monitor cooking and if chicken begins to get too brown, cover pan with foil and continue cooking.

Maple-Glazed Garlic Carrots

Prep time: 5 minutes
Cook time: 15 minutes

Ingredients

3 c. carrots

Nonstick cooking spray

2 cloves garlic

½ c. chopped parsley

3 T. light maple syrup

Salt and pepper

1. Slice carrots into ¼" pieces.

2. Chop garlic cloves and parsley. Set aside.

3. Spray nonstick pan with cooking spray, place all ingredients in the pan and cook over medium heat until carrots reach desired tenderness.

Serves 4
Calories: 64
Fat: 0.2g
Carbohydrates: 15.7g
Protein: 1g

Cucumber & Onion Stuffed Tomatoes

Prep time: 15 minutes
Cook time: No cooking required

Ingredients

4 Roma tomatoes

Salt and pepper

1 c. English cucumber

½ c. red onion

¼ c. dried cranberries

½ T. fresh thyme

1c. ATHENOS nonfat Greek yogurt

1½ T. dry ranch seasoning

1 t. lemon zest

Serves 2
Calories: 136.1
Fat: 1g
Carbohydrates: 20g
Protein: 12.5g

1. Slice tomatoes in half lengthwise and then use a spoon to scoop out seeds and stem area.

2. Salt and pepper inside of tomato halves.

3. Dice cucumber and red onion and chop cranberries and thyme. Set each aside individually.

4. Whisk together yogurt and dry ranch seasoning.

5. Combine cucumbers, onions, salt, pepper and thyme in a bowl.

6. Fold in yogurt dressing, followed by lemon zest and chopped cranberries.

7. Stuff each tomato half with filling mixture, dividing equally. Chill before serving.

Sausage & Feta Stuffed Tomatoes

Prep time: 10 minutes
Cook time: 10 minutes

Ingredients

4 oz. chicken sausage (any flavor)

4 Roma tomatoes

Salt and pepper

4 oz. ATHENOS nonfat feta cheese

Balsamic vinegar

1. Preheat oven to 350 degrees.

2. Dice and brown chicken sausage, cook in skillet until browned. Remove from heat and set aside.

3. Slice tomatoes in half lengthwise and then use a spoon to scoop out seeds and stem area.

4. Salt and pepper inside of tomato halves.

5. Fill tomatoes with browned sausage, dividing evenly.

6. Top each tomato with ½ oz. crumbled feta cheese.

7. Drizzle each with 1 t. balsamic vinegar and season with salt and pepper.

8. Bake for 10 minutes.

Serves 2
Calories: 218.4
Fat: 9.2g
Carbohydrates: 7.8g
Protein: 26.2g

Panko Zucchini

Prep time: 10 minutes
Cook time: 15 minutes

Ingredients

2 medium-sized zucchini

¼ c. liquid egg substitute

¼ c. panko bread crumbs

Onion powder

Garlic powder

Salt and pepper

Serves 2
Calories: 71.3
Fat: 0g
Carbohydrates: 12.3g
Protein: 5.2g

1. Preheat oven to 350 degrees.

2. Cut zucchini into ½" strips.

3. Place zucchini strips, skin side down, on baking sheet.

4. Brush zucchini strips with egg substitute.

5. Sprinkle zucchini with bread crumbs and then season with onion powder, garlic powder, salt and pepper.

6. Bake uncovered for 15 minutes or until tender.

Bread Crumb Baked Asparagus

Prep time: 10 minutes
Cook time: 15 minutes

Ingredients

1 bunch asparagus

¼ c. liquid egg substitute

2 dashes hot sauce

1½ t. brown mustard

⅛ c. bread crumbs

Cayenne pepper

Salt and pepper

1 t. olive oil

3 T. ATHENOS nonfat Greek yogurt

1 t. chopped rosemary

1. Preheat oven to 350 degrees.

2. Snap ends off asparagus and cut stalks in half.

3. Whisk together liquid egg substitute, hot sauce and ½ teaspoon mustard.

4. Add asparagus to mixture and toss to coat.

5. Place asparagus on nonstick baking sheet, individually coat each piece in bread crumbs and place back on sheet.

6. Sprinkle with cayenne pepper and salt and then drizzle with oil.

7. Bake for 15 minutes or until tender.

8. Make dip by whisking together yogurt, remaining mustard and rosemary. Chill before serving.

Serves 2
Asparagus
Calories: 90
Fat: 3g • Carbohydrates: 9.2g
Protein: 6.5g
Dip
Calories: 12
Fat: 0g • Carbohydrates: 1g
Protein: 2.5g

Shana says...

It feels so good to grow things.

When is the last time you planted a garden? You work up the soil, plant your seeds, water them and wait. And you wait. And you go outside and check on the garden…and you wait. You're becoming impatient. You're concerned you did something wrong. You're worried a silly little rabbit or a small bird has ruined your attempt. Then one day, there they are—tiny green sprouts pushing their way through the land. You did it! You cared enough, worked enough and nurtured it enough to help it grow.

Not only does it feel amazing to grow things, but nothing tastes as good as a cucumber fresh from your garden or a tomato you picked right off the vine.

If having your own garden isn't an option, visit your neighborhood farmer's market, join a co-op or visit a local organic farm for the next best thing.

Eating from the soil is beautiful. Grow something and enjoy your harvest with the earthy options I recommend within this chapter!

Balsamic Glazed Pearls & 'Shrooms

Prep time: 10 minutes
Cook time: 10 minutes

Ingredients

30 pearl onions

10 oz. white cap mushrooms

1 clove garlic

1 T. fresh parsley

½ T. Balsamic vinegar

1 t. olive oil

½ T. steak sauce or
Worcestershire sauce

½ T. zero-calorie flavored mustard

Salt and fresh pepper

1. Preheat oven to 350 degrees.

2. Prepare ingredients: Skin pearl onions, cut mushroom caps into quarters, press garlic clove and chop parsley.

3. Whisk together vinegar, olive oil, steak sauce, mustard, salt and pepper.

4. Place all ingredients on jellyroll pan and roll to combine.

5. Bake for 10 minutes.

Serves 2
Calories: 45
Fat: 2g
Carbohydrates: 5g
Protein: 1.5g

Green Bean & Asparagus Casserole

Prep time: 5 to 10 minutes
Cook time: 45 to 60 minutes

Ingredients

3 c. green beans

1½ c. asparagus

⅓ c. onion

1 clove garlic

1 can 98% fat-free
   cream of chicken soup

½ t. dry mustard

¼ t. cumin

Salt and pepper

¼ c. bread crumbs

1 T. olive oil

1. Preheat oven to 350 degrees.

2. Chop green beans, asparagus and onion and place into a bowl.

3. Press garlic clove.

4. Whisk together soup, garlic, mustard, cumin, salt and pepper.

5. Pour soup mixture over vegetables, stir and transfer to 2-quart casserole dish.

6. Stir together bread crumbs and olive oil and then sprinkle over casserole.

7. Bake uncovered 40 to 60 minutes.

Serves 6
Calories: 110
Fat: 4.3g
Carbohydrates: 16g
Protein: 4g

Broccoli & Orzo Bake

Prep time: 5 to 10 minutes
Cook time: 45 to 60 minutes

Ingredients

1 c. cooked orzo

3 c. broccoli florets

$\frac{1}{3}$ c. onion

$\frac{1}{3}$ c. mixed bell pepper

1 oz. Asiago cheese

1 piece light string cheese

1 can 98% fat-free cream of celery soup

1T. zero-calorie flavored mustard

Salt and pepper

1 T. bread crumbs

$\frac{1}{2}$ t. olive oil

1. Preheat oven to 350 degrees.

2. Cook orzo, rinse in cold water and set aside.

3. Prepare ingredients: Chop broccoli, onions and peppers and shred Asiago and string cheese. Set each aside individually.

4. Whisk together soup, mustard, Asiago cheese, salt and pepper.

5. Combine soup mixture with orzo, broccoli, onions and peppers in bowl and transfer to 2-quart casserole dish.

6. Stir together bread crumbs, olive oil and string cheese and then sprinkle over casserole.

7. Bake uncovered 40 to 60 minutes.

Serves 6
Calories: 127
Fat: 4g
Carbohydrates: 18g
Protein: 5.6g

Room for 'Shrooms

Pesto Portabella Puff Pastry

Prep time: 10 to 15 minutes
Cook time: 25 to 30 minutes

Ingredients

1 puff pastry sheet

1 egg white

1 t. basil pesto

6 oz. (6 slices) Canadian bacon

1 portabella mushroom

1 c. spinach

Salt and pepper

Herb salt

½ oz. finely grated Pecorino Romano cheese

1. Roll out pastry onto nonstick baking sheet.

2. Cut pastry in half lengthwise. Set half of pastry sheet aside.

3. Beat egg white and brush over both pieces of pastry.

4. Spread pesto over egg whites.

5. Layer Canadian bacon over pesto.

6. Scrape gills gently and any remainder of stem from mushroom cap, cut mushroom into slices and then layer over bacon.

7. Layer spinach over mushrooms and season with salt and pepper.

8. Place remaining pastry half over layered puff, egg white side down.

9. Sprinkle herb salt on top of pastry, followed by Romano cheese.

10. Bake 25 to 30 minutes, or until pastry is golden brown.

Serves 8
Calories: 173
Fat: 10g
Carbohydrates: 11.5g
Protein: 8g

Spaghetti Stuffed Portabellas

Prep time: 10 minutes
Cook time: 10 minutes

Ingredients

1 c. cooked multicolored corn pasta

8 to 10 portabellini mushrooms

Nonstick cooking spray

Herb salt

Pepper

$1/3$ c. onion

1 clove garlic

10 oz. extra lean ground turkey

¼ c. tomato paste

¼ c. tomato sauce

¼ t. dried basil

¼ t. dried oregano

2 T. grated parmesan cheese

1. Preheat oven to 350 degrees.
2. Cook pasta, rinse in cold water and set aside.
3. Scrape gills gently and any remainder of stem from mushrooms, spray mushrooms with nonstick cooking spray, season with salt and pepper, and bake for 5 minutes. Set aside to cool.
4. Dice onion, press garlic and brown in skillet with ground turkey.
5. Remove from heat and stir in tomato paste, tomato sauce, basil and oregano, followed by cooked pasta.
6. Stuff mushrooms with filling, dividing equally.
7. Top stuffed mushrooms with cheese.
8. Bake mushrooms several minutes until cheese turns golden brown.

Serves 8
Calories: 75
Fat: 1g
Carbohydrates: 7g
Protein: 10.5g

Thai Chicken Stuffed Mushrooms

Prep time: 10 minutes
Cook time: 15 minutes

Ingredients

4 T. cooked cellophane noodles

4 portabella mushrooms

Nonstick cooking spray

Salt and pepper

1 lb. grilled chicken breasts

1 clove garlic

1 T. low-sodium soy sauce

1 T. fresh lemon juice

2 T. Thai peanut sauce

¼ t. fresh grated ginger

Freshly ground black pepper

2 T. green onion

1. Preheat oven to 350 degrees.
2. Cook noodles, rinse in cold water and set aside.
3. Scrape gills gently and any remainder of stem from mushrooms, spray mushrooms with nonstick cooking spray, season with salt and pepper, and bake for 10 minutes. Set aside to cool.
4. Dice grilled chicken breasts and press garlic clove, add to nonstick skillet along with soy sauce, lemon juice, peanut sauce, ginger and pepper, and heat for 3 minutes.
5. Remove from pan, place in bowl and add in diced green onion.
6. Return skillet to stove, add noodles and toss them to coat in any residual sauce from the pan.
7. Stuff mushrooms with chicken filling, dividing equally.
8. Bake mushrooms for 5 minutes, remove from oven and top each with 1 tablespoon noodles before serving.

Serves 4
Calories: 185
Fat: 2.3g
Carbohydrates: 12g
Protein: 27.7g

Crab Salad Bellas

Prep time: 10 minutes
Cook time: 10 minutes

Ingredients

1 c. cooked ready-cut spaghetti noodles

4-oz. can all-white crab meat

6 portabella mushrooms

Nonstick cooking spray

Salt and freshly cracked pepper

4-oz. can medium shrimp

⅓ c. baby peas	¼ t. salt
1½ T. fresh chopped parsley	¼ t. pepper
¼ c. ATHENOS nonfat Greek yogurt	¼ c. Italian bread crumbs
1 T. light mayonnaise	¼ t. olive oil

1. Preheat oven to 350 degrees.
2. Cook noodles, rinse in cold water and set aside.
3. Drain crab meat, squeezing out all liquid, and set aside.
4. Scrape gills gently and any remainder of stem from mushrooms, spray mushrooms with nonstick cooking spray, season with salt and pepper, and bake for 5 minutes. Set aside to cool.
5. Devein shrimp gently under cool running water, if necessary.
6. Stir together crab, peas, 1 tablespoon parsley, yogurt and mayonnaise in bowl.

Serves 3
Calories: 230
Fat: 3.5g
Carbohydrates: 28.2g
Protein: 24g

7. Fold in shrimp gently.
8. Stuff mushrooms with crab filling, dividing equally.
9. Combine bread crumbs, remaining parsley, oil, ¼ teaspoon salt and ¼ teaspoon pepper.
10. Sprinkle bread crumb topping evenly over mushrooms.

Grilled Veggie Stuffed Shrooms

Prep time: 10 minutes
Cook time: 20 minutes

Ingredients

1 zucchini

½ T. olive oil

Salt and pepper

½ c. onion

½ c. red bell pepper

½ c. orange or yellow bell pepper

2 pieces light string cheese

7 asparagus spears

1 t. fresh lemon thyme

12 portabellini mushrooms

Nonstick cooking spray

1 T. balsamic vinegar

1. Preheat oven to 350 degrees.

2. Prepare ingredients: Cut zucchini in half lengthwise, rub with olive oil and season with salt and pepper; slice onions and both peppers; chop asparagus into bite-sized pieces; chop lemon thyme; and grate string cheese. Set each aside individually.

3. Scrape gills gently and any remainder of stem from mushrooms, spray mushrooms with nonstick cooking spray, season with salt and pepper, and bake for 5 minutes. Set aside to cool.

4. Spray grill pan with nonstick cooking spray, place over medium heat with zucchini halves seasoned side down. Grill until desired tenderness and remove from pan.

5. Season remaining veggies with salt and pepper and place in grill pan. Grill until desired tenderness and remove from pan to cool.

6. Cube grilled zucchini and roughly chop other grilled veggies.

7. Combine veggies in bowl with vinegar and remaining olive oil.

8. Stuff mushrooms with veggie filling, dividing equally.

9. Top with cheese, salt and pepper.

10. Bake for 15 minutes.

Serves 3
Calories: 153
Fat: 6.5g
Carbohydrates: 16g
Protein: 10g

Yogurt Stuffed Shrooms

Prep time: 10 minutes
Cook time: 10 minutes

Ingredients

8 oz. mushrooms

1 clove garlic

½ c. onion

1 T. fresh chives

1 T. fresh parsley

2 c. chicken broth

1 c. water

½ c. ATHENOS nonfat Greek yogurt

½ c. fat-free cottage cheese

Salt and pepper

1. Prepare ingredients: Remove stems from mushrooms; press garlic clove; dice onion; and chop chives and parsley.

2. Combine chicken broth, water, garlic and mushrooms in pot.

3. Cook over medium heat until liquid comes to a boil. Remove from burner to cool.

_____

Serves 1
Calories: 107.5
Fat: 4.3g
Carbohydrates: 16.2g
Protein: 25.8g
_____

4. Drain liquid from mushrooms and place them on serving platter.

5. Blend yogurt, cottage cheese, onion, parsley, chives, salt and pepper in food processor or blender until smooth and creamy.

6. Stuff mushrooms with yogurt blend.

7. Season with salt and pepper and garnish with parsley on top.

Spinach & Artichoke Bella Lasagna

Prep time: 10 minutes
Cook time: 30 minutes

Ingredients

12 oz. portabella mushrooms

1 large clove garlic

$\frac{1}{3}$ c. shallots

2 fresh basil

1 T. fresh parsley

13-oz. can spinach

14-oz. can artichoke hearts

1 medium tomato

$\frac{1}{2}$ t. olive oil

1 can 98% fat-free cream of
   mushroom soup

1 c. chicken broth

1¼ c. fat-free ricotta cheese

1¼ c. fat-free cottage cheese

1 egg white

Nonstick cooking spray

1 oz. grated Asiago cheese

1. Preheat oven to 350 degrees.

2. Prepare ingredients: Remove stems and gills from mushrooms and slice;
chop shallots, garlic clove, basil and parsley; drain and squeeze excess liquid from
spinach and artichoke hearts; and dice and remove seeds from tomatoes.

3. Sauté garlic and shallots in olive oil over medium heat.

Spinach & Artichoke Bella Lasagna continued...

4. Add artichoke hearts and spinach and sauté for 5 minutes.

5. Add cream of mushroom soup and chicken broth and heat through.

6. Remove from heat and add basil and tomatoes.

7. Stir together ricotta cheese, cottage cheese, egg white, parsley, salt and pepper in separate bowl.

8. Spray 9" x 13" baking pan with nonstick spray and place layer of mushroom mixture, followed by layer of cheese mixture. Repeat layers a second time.

9. Top with Asiago cheese.

10. Bake uncovered for 30 minutes.

Serves 6
Calories: 181
Fat: 3.5g
Carbohydrates: 22g
Protein: 18g

Tips for Working With Mushrooms

- Don't soak mushrooms. They are porous and will absorb the water.

- If you need to clean them, use a damp cloth or paper towel to rub off any larger chunks of dirt/icky stuff.

- Adding salt and pepper to cooking mushrooms causes them to sweat, which produces moisture that will assist in creating a natural "sauce" of sorts for the additional vegetables/meats that you are cooking with.

- Gilling out a mushroom cap assists with stuffing it by providing a nice area to hold the stuffing in place. Gently break or pop off the stem and scrape the gills out with a spoon.

Pesto & Sundried Tomato Caps

Prep time: 10 minutes
Cook time: 20 to 30 minutes

Ingredients

1 clove garlic

1½ T. rehydrated
    sundried tomatoes

1 T. fresh parsley

8 oz. white cap mushrooms

⅓ c. Italian bread crumbs

1 T. pesto

3 oz. grated Asiago cheese

1. Preheat oven to 350 degrees.

2. Prepare ingredients: Press garlic clove and chop tomatoes and parsley. Set each aside individually.

3. Remove stems from mushrooms, place on baking sheet and set aside.

4. Combine garlic, tomatoes, parsley, bread crumbs, pesto and cheese for filling.

5. Stuff mushrooms with filling, dividing equally.

6. Bake for 20 to 30 minutes.

Serves 5
Calories: 123
Fat: 7.5g
Carbohydrates: 7g
Protein: 7.5g

Mushroom Stuffed Mushrooms

Prep time: 10 minutes
Cook time: 10 to 12 minutes

Ingredients

1 c. cooked wild rice

6 to 8 portabellini mushrooms

Nonstick cooking spray

1 t. olive oil

½ c. red onion

¼ c. red pepper

2 Roma tomatoes

6 oz. variety of sliced mushrooms
   (baby bella, oyster, morel, shitake)

3 oz. ATHENOS nonfat feta cheese

Salt and pepper

1. Preheat oven to 350 degrees.

2. Cook wild rice and set aside.

3. Scrape gills gently and any remainder of stem from mushrooms, spray mushrooms with nonstick cooking spray, season with salt and pepper, and bake for 5 minutes. Set aside to cool.

4. Dice onion, red pepper and tomatoes. Set each aside individually.

5. Place nonstick pan over medium heat, drizzle with olive oil and sauté variety of mushrooms, onion and pepper for 5 to 7 minutes.

6. Stir in cooked rice and remove from heat.

7. Stuff mushrooms with rice-mushroom mixture, dividing evenly.

8. Top each mushroom with diced tomatoes, ½ ounce crumbled feta, salt and pepper.

Serves 6
Calories: 100
Fat: 3g
Carbohydrates: 13g
Protein: 6g

Room for 'Shrooms

Cream of Mushroom Soup

Prep time: 5 minutes
Cook time: 20 minutes

Ingredients

2 T. red onion

1½ T. shallot

½ c. leek

1 clove garlic

1 c. rehydrated specialty mushrooms

2 c. white cap mushrooms

2 fresh bay leaves

2 large sprigs thyme

1 can 98% fat-free cream of
    chicken or cream of celery soup

2 c. chicken or vegetable broth

1. Prepare ingredients: Chop onion, shallot and leek (avoid most of green portion); press garlic clove; and reserve stock from rehydrated mushrooms.

2. Combine onions, shallots, garlic, both types mushrooms, leeks, bay leaves, thyme, salt, pepper and reserved mushroom stock in soup pot and simmer for 10 minutes.

3. Remove thyme sprigs and bay leaves.

4. Add soup and chicken broth and simmer another 10 minutes before serving.

Variation: Add rice or diced grilled chicken for a little extra heartiness.

Serves 4
Calories: 80
Fat: 2.4g
Carbohydrates: 12g
Protein: 4g

Spectacular Spuds

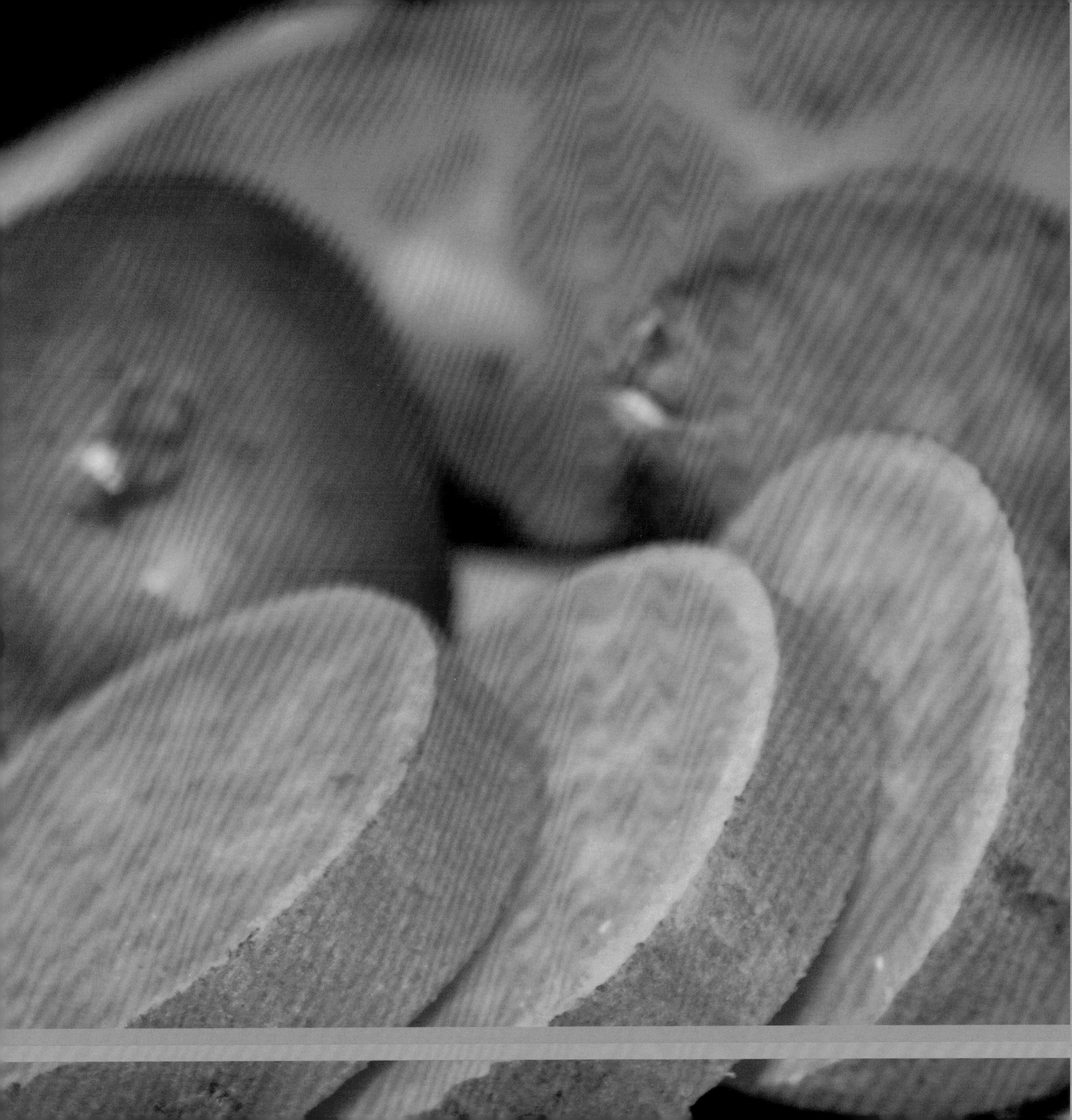

Rosemary Reds With Pearl Onions

Prep time: 5 to 10 minutes
Cook time: 40 to 45 minutes

Ingredients

4 medium baby red potatoes

20 pearl onions

1 T. garlic-flavored olive oil

½ T. fresh rosemary

Salt and pepper

1. Preheat oven to 350 degrees.

2. Dice potatoes into ½" cubes.

3. Cut ends off onions and remove first layer of skin.

4. Place potatoes and onions on jellyroll pan and drizzle with olive oil.

5. Chop fresh rosemary and add to pan, along with salt and pepper.

6. Toss until potatoes are thoroughly covered with seasonings.

7. Bake 45 minutes or until potatoes are tender.

Serves 5
Calories: 158
Fat: 2.9g
Carbohydrates: 30.6g
Protein: 3.6g

Fried Reds With Mixed Peppers

Prep time: 5 to 10 minutes
Cook time: 30 to 40 minutes

Ingredients

2 large red potatoes

2 c. bell peppers
(any desired colors)

2 green onions
(about ½ c. diced)

1 T. olive oil
Salt and pepper

Serves 5
Calories: 148
Fat: 3g
Carbohydrates: 28.3g
Protein: 3.5g

1. Cut potatoes in half and then into thin slices.

2. Slice peppers into strips and dice green onions.

3. Place nonstick pan over medium heat, drizzle with olive oil, add potatoes, peppers and onions.

4. Fry for 30 to 40 minutes, stirring often, until potatoes are tender.

5. Season with salt and pepper to taste.

Greek Mashers

Prep time: 5 minutes
Cook time: 30 to 40 minutes

Ingredients

4 medium potatoes

1 small shallot

1 t. crushed red pepper

½ c. vegetable broth

2 T. hummus

2 oz. ATHENOS nonfat
feta cheese

Salt and pepper

1 T. fresh chives

1. Boil potatoes, drain off water and mash to desired consistency in bowl. Set aside.

2. Mince shallot and chives. Set aside each individually.

3. Place small amount of vegetable broth in skillet over medium heat and sauté shallots and red pepper flakes for 2 to 3 minutes. Remove from heat and let cool slightly.

4. Pour pan ingredients into mashed potatoes and mix together.

5. Add additional vegetable broth until potatoes are creamy.

6. Add 1 tablespoon hummus and 1 ounce feta cheese for every ¾ cup mashed potatoes. Mix well.

Serving size: 1 c.
Calories: 206
Fat: 6.4g
Carbohydrates: 30g
Protein: 9.6g

Spectacular Spuds

Corn & Salsa Mashers

Prep time: 10 minutes
Cook time: 20 to 25 minutes

Ingredients

5 medium Yukon Gold potatoes
   (2 c. mashed)

½ c. chicken broth

½ c. ATHENOS nonfat
   Greek yogurt

⅓ c. green onion

½ t. fresh thyme

1 c. white and gold corn

½ c. nonfruit salsa of choice

Salt and pepper

Serves 4
Calories: 127
Fat: 1.1g
Carbohydrates: 25.6g
Protein: 6.9g

1. Boil potatoes, drain off water and mash to desired consistency in bowl. Set aside.

2. Stir in chicken broth and yogurt to desired creaminess.

3. Chop green onions and thyme and add to potatoes.

4. Fold in corn, salsa, salt and pepper.

Chipotle Mashed Potatoes

Prep time: 10 to 15 minutes
Cook time: 35 to 45 minutes

Ingredients

2½ lb. Yukon Gold potatoes

Salt

Nonstick cooking spray

½ medium onion

½ c. mushrooms

1T. chopped chipotle pepper in adobo sauce

1t. fresh thyme

1T. parsley

1 c. vegetable broth

1 T. diced green chilies

½ T. adobo sauce

½ c. ATHENOS nonfat Greek yogurt

1. Cube potatoes, boil in salt water until tender, drain off water and mash to desired consistency in bowl.

2. Prepare ingredients: Dice onions, mushrooms and pepper and mince thyme and parsley. Set each aside individually.

3. Spray nonstick pan with cooking spray, add onions, mushrooms and ½ cup chicken broth and sauté until onions are tender. Remove from heat and set aside.

Shana says...

Potatoes have gotten a bad rap. It's not that they are awful for you; it's just that people are often under the impression that they are a vegetable.

True, potatoes grow among the vegetables, but they are a starch. They are more similar to rice, pasta, breads and other grains than they would be to broccoli. For that reason, and because a potato's typical accompaniments are butter, sour cream and cheese, people tend to shy away from potatoes when trying to eat healthy.

No need to cut potatoes out of your diet completely! Follow these few simple tips:

- Keep in mind that potatoes are a starch and eat them with an additional vegetable, such as green beans, spinach, cauliflower, etc.

- Top potatoes with lighter options than sour cream and butter, such as Athenos nonfat Greek yogurt, Athenos nonfat feta cheese, salt and pepper, salsa or marinara sauce.

- Be sure to stick to serving sizes: For example, 1 exchange is 3 ounces of baked potato and 2 ounces of baked sweet potato.

- Use chicken or vegetable broth to loosen mashed potatoes rather than butter and milk.

- Stay away from deep-fried potato options!

Chipotle Mashed Potatoes continued...

4. Mix chilies, chipotle pepper and adobo sauce into potatoes.

5. Fold onion-mushroom mixture into potatoes.

6. Stir in yogurt, parsley and thyme.

7. Mix thoroughly until desired creaminess, adding in more chicken broth, if necessary.

8. Season with salt and pepper to taste.

Serves 6
Calories: 157.7
Fat: 1g
Carbohydrates: 32.2g
Protein: 7g

Golden Sweets

Prep time: 10 to 15 minutes
Cook time: 40 to 45 minutes

Ingredients

2 large sweet potatoes
3 medium Yukon Gold potatoes
Vegetable broth
1 T. fresh chives
½ T. fresh rosemary
½ T. fresh thyme
½ c. ATHENOS nonfat Greek yogurt
½ t. fresh ground red pepper
Fresh ground black pepper
Salt

1. Cube sweet potatoes and boil in salt water until tender.

2. Cube potatoes, boil in separate pan until tender, drain off water and place in bowl.

3. Drain water from sweet potatoes, remove skins and place in bowl with other potatoes.

4. Mash by hand until desired consistency, adding chicken broth as needed.

5. Mince chives, rosemary and thyme.

6. Whisk herbs together with yogurt, freshly ground red pepper, black pepper and salt, and stir into mashed potatoes.

Serves 5
Calories: 169.8
Fat: 4g
Carbohydrates: 36.3g
Protein: 6.5g

Baked Cinnamon Sweets

Prep time: 5 to 10 minutes
Cook time: 30 to 35 minutes

Ingredients

2 medium sweet potatoes
1 T. light syrup
¼ c. raisins
⅛ t. pumpkin pie spice
⅛ t. allspice
¼ T. cinnamon
¾ T. no-calorie sweetener
Salt and pepper

1. Preheat oven to 350 degrees.

2. Peel sweet potatoes and cut into 1" cubes (3 cups total).

3. Place sweet potatoes on jellyroll pan and drizzle with syrup.

4. Sprinkle with raisins and dry ingredients.

5. Bake for 30 minutes or until potatoes are tender.

6. Season with salt and pepper to taste.

Serves 4
Calories: 121
Fat: 0.3g
Carbohydrates: 28.6g
Protein: 2g

Sweet Potato Soup

Prep time: 5 minutes
Cook time: 10 minutes

Ingredients

3 medium sweet potatoes
    (about 4 c. cooked)

Salt

½ t. ginger

½ t. cinnamon

½ t. nutmeg

½ T. no-calorie sweetener

Salt and pepper

Vegetable broth

¼ c. ATHENOS nonfat Greek yogurt

6 t. chopped pecans

1 T. no-calorie brown sugar

1. Cube sweet potatoes and boil in salt water until tender.

2. Drain off water, let cool, remove skins and place in soup pot.

3. Add ginger, cinnamon, nutmeg, no-calorie sweetener, vegetable broth and yogurt, and blend together with hand mixer.

4. Cook on low heat until warmed through.

5. Garnish with 1 teaspoon chopped pecans and a pinch of brown sugar.

Serves 6
Calories: 160
Fat: 7g
Carbohydrates: 22.5g
Protein: 4g

Feta & Mushroom Reds

Prep time: 5 minutes
Cook time: 5 minutes

Ingredients

½ c. red potatoes

2 c. mushrooms

½ c. onion

1 clove garlic

1 sprig thyme

¼ c. chicken broth

Salt and pepper

1 oz. ATHENOS nonfat feta cheese

1. Cube potatoes, boil in salt water until tender, drain off water and place on serving plate.

2. Prepare ingredients: Slice mushrooms, dice onions, press garlic clove and mince thyme sprig.

Serves 1
Calories: 180
Fat: 4.8g
Carbohydrates: 24.8g
Protein: 13g

3. Sauté mushrooms, onions, garlic and thyme with chicken broth in skillet over medium heat.

4. Remove from heat and season with salt and pepper.

5. Pour skillet mixture over potatoes.

6. Top with crumbled feta cheese.

Variation: Add diced grilled chicken for a complete meal.

Chicken & Broccoli Yukon Golds

Prep time: 10 minutes
Cook time: 10 minutes

Ingredients

4 oz. Yukon Gold potato

4 oz. chicken breast

1 T. chicken broth

1 c. broccoli florets

½ T. fresh sage

⅛ t. fresh rosemary

1 piece light string cheese

1. Boil potato in salt water until tender, drain off water and place on plate to cool.

2. Prepare ingredients: Steam broccoli until tender; mince sage and rosemary; and shred string cheese. Set each aside individually.

3. Grill chicken in nonstick skillet over medium heat, using chicken broth to prevent burning. Cook until juices run clear.

4. Remove chicken from heat, let cool slightly and dice into bite-sized pieces.

5. Place chicken, broccoli and herbs into pan and cook for 2 minutes, using additional chicken broth if needed.

6. Place chicken-broccoli blend over potato and sprinkle with shredded cheese.

Serves 1
Calories: 256
Fat: 4.3g
Carbohydrates: 19g
Protein: 36g

Feelin' Fishy

Crabby Avocado Haddock

Prep time: 15 to 20 minutes
Cook time: 30 to 40 minutes

Ingredients

12-oz. haddock fillet

½ c. chicken broth

Salt and pepper

4 T. onion

Fresh dill sprigs

1 t. diced jalapenos

½ c. imitation crab meat

½ T. fresh dill

1 lime

½ medium avocado

½ T. rehydrated sundried tomato

1. Preheat oven to 350 degrees.
2. Cut haddock fillet in half and place in glass baking dish.
3. Season with salt, pepper and 2 tablespoons minced onion.
4. Lay fresh dill over fish.
5. Bake uncovered for 30 minutes, or until fish flakes with fork.

Avocado-Crab Blend

1. Prepare ingredients: Mince crab meat, onion and dill; juice lime; and chop avocado and sundried tomatoes.
2. Stir together jalapenos, crab, 2 tablespoons onion, lime juice, and tomatoes.
3. Fold in avocado gently.
4. Top each fish fillet with even distribution of blend topping.

Serves 3
Fish Fillet
Calories: 126.9
Fat: 1.1g • Carbohydrates: 0g
Protein: 27.5g
Avocado-Crab Blend
Calories: 83.2
Fat: 5.1g • Carbohydrates: 8.1g
Protein: 2.4g

Funky Fish Tacos

Prep time: 5 to 10 minutes
Cook time: 10 minutes

Ingredients

1 T. olive oil

2 4-oz. orange roughy fillets

Salt and pepper

Red bell pepper

Small onion

3 low-carb whole wheat tortillas

¼ c. ATHENOS nonfat Greek yogurt

1 T. dill relish

¼ t. paprika

¼ t. salt

⅛ t. pepper

1 T. medium to hot salsa

Serves 3
Calories: 218.4
Fat: 8g
Carbohydrates: 17g
Protein: 24g

1. Drizzle olive oil in skillet over medium heat and place fish fillets in oil when warm.

2. Season fillets with salt and pepper, cook until bottom turns golden brown, flip fillet and repeat with salt and pepper seasoning. Fillet is done cooking when it flakes with fork.

3. Thinly slice onion and pepper, and assemble tacos in tortillas.

4. Whisk together yogurt, dill, paprika, salt, pepper and salsa to create tartar salsa. Serve on the side.

Seafood Stuffed Cod

Prep time: 15 to 20 minutes
Cook time: 30 to 45 minutes

Serves 3
Calories: 200
Fat: 3.8g
Carbohydrates: 8.9g
Protein: 31.1g

Main Ingredients
12 oz. cod fillet
2 T. chicken broth
Salt and pepper
2 T. minced onion
Fresh dill sprigs
1 clove garlic

Crab-Veggie Stuffing Ingredients
½ t. olive oil
2 T. celery
2 T. red bell pepper
1 clove garlic
½ c. imitation crab meat
Salt and pepper
 ¼ c. chicken broth
½ c. stuffing mix
½ oz. grated Asiago cheese

1. Preheat oven to 350 degrees.
2. Cut cod fillet in half and place in glass baking dish.
3. Season with salt, pepper, 2 tablespoons minced onion and pressed garlic clove.
4. Lay fresh dill over fish.
5. Bake uncovered for 30 minutes, or until fish flakes with fork.

Crab-Veggie Stuffing
1. Prepare ingredients: Dice celery, bell pepper and carrots; press garlic clove; and mince crab meat. Set each aside individually.
2. Drizzle olive oil in skillet over medium heat and sauté celery, pepper, garlic, crab, salt and pepper for 3 to 5 minutes.
3. Add chicken broth and stuffing mix.
4. Remove from heat, cover and let stand for 5 minutes.

Bring It Together

1. Place fish on plate.

2. Discard liquid in baking dish and wipe out.

3. Portion fish into 3 servings and place back into dish.

4. Spoon crab-veggie stuffing over fillets, dividing equally.

5. Top with Asiago cheese.

6. Bake until cheese is melted.

Shana says...

White fish is fabulous, and it's so simple to make! Bake it with a little salt and pepper. Boil it in water for "poor man's lobster," and enjoy it with a bit of lemon juice. Or try this killer recipe!

Remember: Eating fish twice per week will increase your health by lowering your bad cholesterol (LDL) and increasing the HDL. And, white fish is seriously low in calories!

Cheddar Cracker-Encrusted Cod

Prep time: 5 minutes
Cook time: 25 to 30 minutes

Ingredients

¼ c. chicken broth
Juice of 1 lemon
2 sprigs fresh rosemary
2 4-oz. cod fillets
1 t. olive oil
Salt and pepper
¼ c. cheddar crackers

1. Preheat oven to 350 degrees.

2. Cover bottom of 9" square baking dish with chicken broth.

3. Squeeze juice of a lemon into broth.

4. Add sprigs of rosemary.

5. Place cod fillets into dish, use finger to rub each with ½ teaspoon olive oil and season with salt and pepper.

6. Crush crackers and sprinkle evenly over fish fillets.

7. Bake for 25 to 30 minutes, or until fish flakes with fork.

Serves 3
Calories: 155
Fat: 2.9g
Carbohydrates: 4.3g
Protein: 26.6g

Feelin' Fishy

Grilled Ahi Tuna Sandwich

Prep time: 5 minutes
Cook time: 30 minutes

Ingredients

1 t. olive oil

3-oz. Ahi tuna steak

1 T. liquid egg substitute

1 T. panko bread crumbs

2 T. ATHENOS nonfat Greek yogurt

1 t. pickle relish

1 t. wasabi mustard

¼ t. low-sodium soy sauce

Low-carb whole wheat bun

Lettuce

1. Drizzle skillet with olive oil and place over medium heat.

Serves 1 (with bun)
Calories: 273
Fat: 8g
Carbohydrates: 20g
Protein: 32.2g

2. Coat both sides of tuna steak in egg substitute and bread crumbs.

3. Place breaded tuna steak in hot oil, season with salt and pepper, heat until bottom turns brown and flip to heat other side until brown.

4. Remove tuna steak from pan and prepare wasabi tartar sauce.

5. Stir together yogurt, pickle relish, wasabi mustard and soy sauce.

6. Serve tuna steak on whole wheat bun with lettuce and wasabi tartar sauce.

Shrimp Scampi

Prep time: 5 minutes
Cook time: 5 minutes

Ingredients

1 lb. shrimp

2 c. cooked pasta

1 clove garlic

1 shallot

2 T. fresh parsley

1 T. olive oil

¼ c. chicken broth

1 T. lemon juice

½ T. apple cider vinegar

Salt and pepper

1. Thaw and thoroughly drain shrimp.

2. Cook pasta, rinse in cold water and set aside.

3. Prepare ingredients: Mince garlic and finely chop shallot and parsley. Set each aside individually.

4. Drizzle olive oil in nonstick pan, place over medium heat, add garlic, shallot, chicken broth, lemon juice and vinegar, and heat until warm.

5. Add in shrimp and parsley, season with salt and pepper and simmer just a few minutes until shrimp is warmed through.

6. Toss, remove from heat and serve over cooked noodles.

Serves 1
Calories: 216
Fat: 5g
Carbohydrates: 16g
Protein: 27g

Feelin' Fishy

Tuna Pasta Bake

Prep time: 10 to 15 minutes
Cook time: 15 to 20 minutes

Ingredients

2 c. cooked pasta

2 5-oz. cans light tuna in water

½ c. mushrooms

1 Roma tomato

¼ c. onion

½ T. garlic

Salt and pepper

2 oz. ATHENOS nonfat feta cheese

1½ T. Dijon mustard

Louisiana hot sauce to taste

1 T. bread crumbs

Nonstick cooking spray

Serves 3
Calories: 212
Fat: 3.7g
Carbohydrates: 23g
Protein: 22.9g

1. Preheat oven to 350 degrees.

2. Cook pasta, rinse in cold water and set aside.

3. Prepare ingredients: Drain tuna; chop mushrooms, tomatoes and onion; and press garlic. Set each aside individually.

4. Drizzle nonstick pan with olive oil, place over medium heat and sauté vegetables with salt and pepper for 3 to 5 minutes. Remove from heat to cool.

5. Combine pasta, tuna, vegetables, feta, mustard and hot sauce in bowl.

6. Place mixture in 2-quart casserole dish and top with bread crumbs.

7. Spray bread crumbs with nonstick cooking spray and place casserole dish in oven to bake for 15 to 20 minutes until golden brown.

Yogurt Herbed Tilapia

Prep time: 5 to 10 minutes
Cook time: 20 to 25 minutes

Ingredients

1 clove garlic

¼ c. onion

1 T. dill

2 T. parsley

12-oz. tilapia fillet

¼ c. vegetable broth

2 T. ATHENOS nonfat
  Greek yogurt

Salt and pepper

1. Preheat oven to 350 degrees.

2. Prepare ingredients: Press garlic; dice onion; and chop dill and parsley. Set each aside individually.

3. Form an aluminum boat with foil and place tilapia fillet inside.

4. Pour vegetable broth over fish.

5. Mix together yogurt, onion and garlic, and spread over fish.

6. Season with salt, pepper, dill and parsley.

7. Cover boat with another sheet of foil, fold over edges and place in oven to bake for 20 to 25 minutes.

Serves 3
Calories: 132
Fat: 3g
Carbohydrates: 2g
Protein: 25.5g

Feelin' Fishy

Baked Scallops

Prep time: 10 to 15 minutes
Cook time: 5 to 7 minutes

Ingredients

¼ c. diced tomatoes

1 T. fresh parsley

1 T. fresh dill

¼ c. chicken broth

12 oz. scallops

1 t. olive oil

Salt and pepper

Serves 2
Calories: 177
Fat: 3.5g
Carbohydrates: 5.5g
Protein: 29g

1. Preheat oven to 500 degrees.

2. Prepare ingredients: Drain tomatoes and chop parsley and dill. Set each aside individually.

3. Make a circle with diced tomatoes in the bottom of a 9" square glass baking dish.

4. Pour chicken broth into the center of the tomato ring and place scallops inside the broth.

5. Drizzle with olive oil and season with salt, pepper, parsley and dill.

6. Bake 5 to 7 minutes, or until scallops are just cooked through.

Stuffed Shells With Seafood Sauce

Prep time: 20 minutes plus overnight chilling
Cook time: 1 hour 20 minutes

Ingredients

2 oz. cooked jumbo shells	½ t. fennel
4-oz. can crab (15% leg meat)	1 t. no-calorie
1 c. diced tomatoes	sweetener
2 T. red pepper	½ c. vegetable broth
2 T. green pepper	⅔ c. tomato sauce
2 T. shallot	Salt and pepper
2 T. garlic	½ c. fat-free
¾ T. Serrano pepper	cottage cheese
1 T. lemon-and-herb seafood seasoning	
½ t. basil	½ c. fat-free ricotta
½ t. oregano	1 egg white
½ c. reduced-fat Italian cheese	1 T. parsley

Serves 3
Calories: 226
Fat: 2.6g
Carbohydrates: 26g
Protein: 25.6g

1. Cook shells for 9 minutes, rinse and set aside.
2. Prepare ingredients: Drain and squeeze crab meat; drain diced tomatoes; mince red pepper, green pepper, shallot, garlic and Serrano pepper; and chop basil, oregano and parsley. Set each aside individually.
3. Combine crab, tomatoes, red, green and Serrano peppers, shallots, garlic, seafood seasoning, basil, oregano, fennel, no-calorie sweetener, vegetable broth, tomato sauce, salt and pepper to create sauce. Simmer over medium heat for 20 minutes.
4. Combine cottage cheese, ricotta, egg white and parsley for stuffing and stuff in shells evenly.
5. Place shells in 9" square glass baking dish and pour sauce over the shells.
6. Sprinkle shells with cheese, cover pan and refrigerate overnight.
7. Turn oven to 350 degrees, place cold dish into oven and bake uncovered for 60 minutes.

Feelin' Fishy

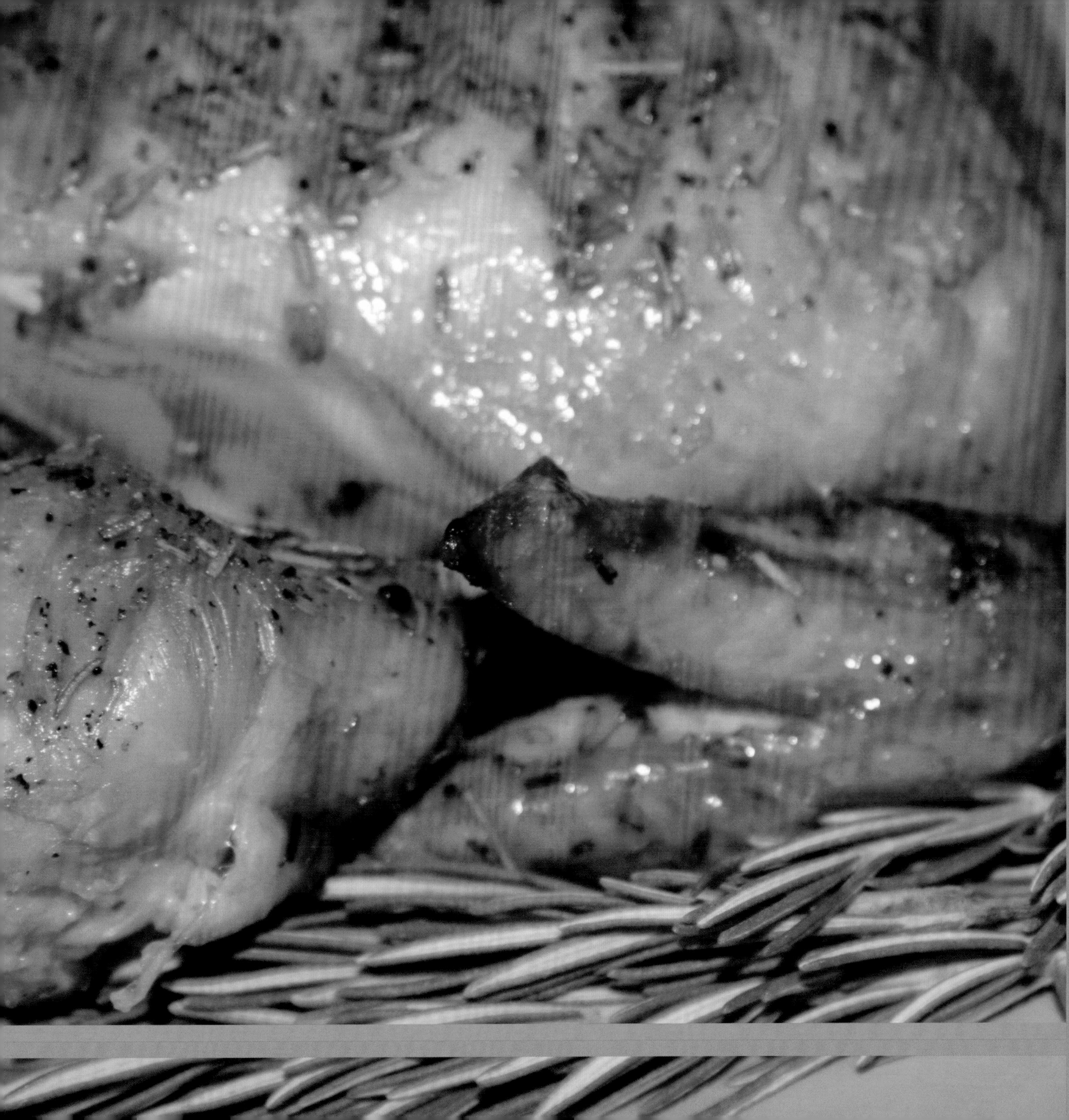

The Bird's the Word

Chicken Pockets

Prep time: 20 minutes
Cook time: 15 minutes

Ingredients

1 pkg. crescent rolls

Nonstick cooking spray

5-oz. can chicken in water

¼ c. chopped green pepper

1 stalk celery chopped

¼ c. fresh mushrooms diced

1 clove minced garlic

1 T. spicy mustard

½ t. dried basil

Salt and pepper

½ c. ATHENOS nonfat Greek yogurt

1 t. dried minced onion

½ T. olive oil

Serves 6
Calories: 201 • Fat: 6.5g
Carbohydrates: 20g • Protein: 18g

1. Preheat oven to 350 degrees.
2. Unroll crescent roll dough and divide into 12 equal parts.
3. Spray baking sheet with cooking spray and press out each piece of dough, flattening as much as possible into squares.
4. Dice green pepper, celery, mushrooms and garlic, and mix together in bowl with chicken.
5. Whisk together mustard, basil, salt, pepper, yogurt and dried minced onion, and fold into chicken-veggie mixture.
6. Divide filling mixture evenly among all 12 dough squares.
7. Bring corners to center and pinch together, forming pockets.
8. Use finger to rub olive oil on top of each pocket and season with salt and pepper.
9. Bake for 15 to 18 minutes, or until golden brown.

Feta & Asparagus Stuffed Chicken

Prep time: 10 minutes
Cook time: 30 to 40 minutes

Ingredients
Nonstick cooking spray
3 5-oz. chicken breasts
Salt and pepper
3 oz. ATHENOS nonfat feta cheese
9 asparagus spears

Serves 3
Calories: 206
Fat: 5.6g
Carbohydrates: 1.6g
Protein: 35.9g

1. Preheat oven to 350 degrees.

2. Soak 10 toothpicks in water for 10 minutes.

3. Place chicken breasts between two pieces plastic wrap and pound to ¼" thickness.

4. Spray 2-quart baking dish with nonstick cooking spray and place chicken breasts inside.

5. Season chicken with salt and pepper and crumble feta on top.

6. Lay three asparagus spears on each chicken breast.

7. Roll chicken around asparagus and feta, securing with toothpicks as needed, and season with salt and pepper.

8. Bake uncovered for 30 to 40 minutes, or until chicken is cooked through.

Skinny Chicken Pot Pie

Prep time: 15 minutes
Cook time: 30 minutes

Ingredients

1.25 lbs. chicken breast

½ c. onion

4 stalks celery

1 c. carrots

4 green onions

2 cloves garlic

½ of Anaheim chili pepper

Hot sauce to taste

Salt and pepper

1 can 98% fat-free
   cream of mushroom soup

1 pastry shell

1. Preheat oven to 350 degrees.
2. Prepare ingredients: Dice onions; chop celery, carrots, green onions and chili pepper; and press garlic cloves. Set each aside individually.
3. Spray nonstick pan with cooking spray and cook chicken over medium heat until juices run clear.
4. Remove from pan, let cool slightly and dice into bite-sized pieces.
5. Return diced chicken to pan, add in remaining ingredients (except for soup and pastry shell) and cook 5 to 10 minutes.
6. Remove from heat, stir in soup and pour into 9" x 11" baking dish.
7. Roll out pastry shell, place on top of chicken mixture and season with salt and pepper.
8. Bake for 30 minutes or until pastry shell is golden brown.

Serves 6
Calories: 327
Fat: 13g
Carbohydrates: 23g
Protein: 26g

Lemon & Roasted Pepper Chicken

Prep time: 10 minutes
Cook time: 20 to 25 minutes

Ingredients

Handful fresh spinach

Zest and juice of 1 lemon

1 clove garlic

1 fire-roasted red pepper

1 t. herb salt

1 t. black pepper

¼ c. aged balsamic vinegar

Nonstick cooking spray

1.25 lbs. chicken breast

1. Place spinach, lemon zest and juice, garlic, red pepper, herb salt, pepper and vinegar in food processor and blend well to create marinade.

2. Place chicken breast in bowl, pour marinade over the top, cover and let marinate in refrigerator overnight.

3. Spray nonstick skillet with cooking spray, place over medium heat and cook chicken and marinade together until center of chicken breast is no longer pink.

Serves 5
Calories: 140.5
Fat: 1.5g
Carbohydrates: 3.7g
Protein: 26.6g

Spicy Turkey Sandwiches

Prep time: 5 to 10 minutes
Cook time: 7 hours

Ingredients

20-oz. peppered turkey tenderloin

1 packet dry French onion soup mix

1½ c. pickle juice

2 T. diced jalapenos

4 c. water

½ c. ATHENOS nonfat Greek yogurt

1 T. yellow mustard

Salt and pepper

1. Place tenderloin, soup mix, pickle juice, jalapenos and water in slow cooker and heat on high for at least 7 hours.

2. Remove tenderloin and shred with forks in a bowl.

3. Scoop out all onions and peppers and then whisk together ½ cup slow cooker liquid with yogurt, mustard, salt and pepper.

4. Fold turkey into sauce and enjoy as a sandwich meat, over pasta or as a baked potato topper.

Serves 1
Calories: 200
Fat: 4.5g
Carbohydrates: 24.8g
Protein: 33g

Spinach & Chicken Sausage Pasta

Prep time: 5 minutes
Cook time: 10 minutes

Ingredients

1 c. cooked pasta

12 oz. chicken sausage (any flavor)

1 clove garlic

1 tomato

$\frac{1}{3}$ c. onion

1 t. fresh basil
Salt and pepper

2 c. fresh spinach

1 T. water

Serves 3
Calories: 239
Fat: 10g
Carbohydrates: 14g
Protein: 25.1g

1. Cook pasta, rinse in cold water and set aside.

2. Prepare ingredients: Slice chicken sausage into bite-sized pieces; press garlic; dice tomato; and chop onion and basil.

3. Place all prepared ingredients, along with olive oil, salt and pepper, in skillet (only pasta, spinach and water are initially left out) and sauté for 5 to 7 minutes over medium heat.

4. Add spinach and water to skillet, cook until spinach is wilted and remove from heat.

5. Toss sausage-veggie mixture with pasta and serve.

Buffalo Chicken Pasta

Prep time: 5 minutes
Cook time: 10 minutes

Ingredients

½ c. cooked pasta

3-oz. chicken breast

2 T. Feta-Yogurt Dip
(see page 29)

1 t. Louisiana hot sauce

1. Cook pasta, rinse in cold water and set aside.

2. Grill chicken breast in nonstick skillet until juices run clear, remove from heat and dice chicken into bite-sized pieces when cooled.

3. Combine all ingredients together.

Serves 1
Calories: 191
Fat: 2.4g
Carbohydrates: 15.7g
Protein: 26.5g

Grilled Chicken Flatbread Sandwich

Prep time: 5 minutes
Cook time: 10 minutes

Ingredients

1 T. onion

1 tomato

1 piece light string cheese

¼ t. fresh rosemary

3-oz. chicken breast

Salt and pepper

1 T. ATHENOS nonfat Greek yogurt

½ T. yellow mustard

¼ t. pesto

1 light flatbread

1. Prepare ingredients: Thinly slice onion and tomato; grate string cheese; and chop rosemary.

2. Season both sides of chicken breast with salt and pepper and grill until juices run clear. Remove from heat to cool.

3. Whisk together yogurt, mustard and pesto and spread mixture onto half of the flatbread.

4. Lay onions over the sauce.

5. Slice chicken into strips and place over onions.

6. Add tomato slices, rosemary, grated cheese, salt and pepper.

7. Fold flatbread over and heat on Panini press, stove or grill.

Serves 1
Calories: 244
Fat: 6g
Carbohydrates: 17g
Protein: 33.2g

Chicken & Basil Pizza

Prep time: 5 minutes
Cook time: 15 minutes

Ingredients

2 T. ATHENOS nonfat Greek yogurt

1 T. marinara sauce

1/8 t. oregano

1 pinch ground fennel

1 pinch ground cumin

1/4 t. dry ranch seasoning

1 piece light flatbread

3-oz. grilled chicken breast

1 T. fresh basil

1/4 c. spinach leaves

1/4 c. mushrooms

1/2 oz. Asiago cheese

1. Preheat oven to 350 degrees.

2. Whisk together yogurt, marinara sauce and seasonings.

3. Spread sauce mixture over flatbread.

4. Chop chicken breast and basil, tear spinach leaves, slice mushrooms and sprinkle onto flatbread.

5. Top with grated Asiago cheese.

6. Bake until cheese turns golden brown.

Serves 1
Calories: 265.6
Fat: 8.4g
Carbohydrates: 15.6g
Protein: 35.6g

Chicken & Orzo Stuffed Tomatoes

Prep time: 5 to 10 minutes
Cook time: No cooking required

Ingredients

1 c. cooked orzo

3 medium tomatoes

1 c. cucumbers

2 T. onions

1 clove garlic

¼ t. fresh oregano

¼ t. fresh basil

½ T. fresh parsley

9 oz. canned white chicken

1 T. olive oil

½ t. white wine vinegar

½ t. mustard

¼ c. chicken broth

Salt and pepper

Serves 3
Calories: 220
Fat: 6.3g
Carbohydrates: 17.5g
Protein: 22.8g

1. Cook orzo, rinse in cold water and set aside.
2. Cut off tops of tomatoes, use spoon to remove seeds and set aside hollowed-out tomatoes.
3. Prepare ingredients: Dice cucumber and onion; press garlic; chop oregano, basil and parsley. Set each aside individually.
4. Combine orzo, chicken, cucumbers and onions in a bowl.
5. Whisk together olive oil, vinegar, mustard, chicken broth, salt and pepper in a separate bowl.
6. Pour dressing over chicken-veggie-orzo mixture and stir to combine.
7. Divide evenly and stuff tomatoes.

Chicken With Spicy Honey Dip

Prep time: 5 minutes
Cook time: 10 minutes

Ingredients

8-oz. chicken breast

Salt and pepper

Nonstick cooking spray

1 T. natural peanut butter

½ T. honey

½ T. chili sauce

1 T. low-sodium soy sauce

⅛ t. ground ginger

1 t. to 1 T. water

1. Cut chicken into strips and season both sides with salt and pepper.

2. Spray nonstick pan with cooking spray, place over medium heat and cook chicken strips until juices run clear.

3. Whisk together remaining ingredients and pour over chicken in the pan. Use water to loosen sauce from pan bottom, if needed.

4. Remove pan from heat, place chicken on plate, drizzle lightly with sauce and reserve remaining sauce on side for dipping.

Serves 2
Calories: 205
Fat: 5.4g
Carbohydrates: 6g
Protein: 29.2g

Note: This recipe is the winner of the Facebook recipe challenge in which fans supplied three ingredients for Shana to use to create a unique dish for the book. Big thanks to Jen K. of Appleton, Wis., for the inspiration!

Rice Noodles With Peanut Sauce

Prep time: 5 minutes
Cook time: No cooking required

Ingredients

1 c. cooked rice noodles

1 T. natural peanut butter

1 t. zero-calorie flavored mustard

2 T. low-sodium soy sauce

2 T. fresh-squeezed orange juice

1 green onion

1. Cook noodles, rinse in cold water and set aside.

2. Whisk together peanut butter, mustard, soy sauce and orange juice to create sauce.

3. Combine sauce and noodles.

4. Mince green onion and sprinkle on top for garnish.

Serves 2
Calories: 168
Fat: 4.5g
Carbohydrates: 23.9g
Protein: 6.2g

Sweet & Sour Pork

Prep time: 10 minutes
Cook time: 15 minutes

Ingredients

2 c. cooked long grain white rice

Nonstick cooking spray

1 lb. pork tenderloin

10 baby carrots

2 celery stalks

1 clove garlic

⅓ c. onions, sliced

3 c. mushrooms, sliced

½ c. broccoli slaw

1 c. bean sprouts

1 T. wasabi mustard

2 T. low-sodium soy sauce

4 T. sweet-and-sour sauce

1 green onion

1. Cook white rice and set aside.
2. Prepare ingredients: Cube pork tenderloin; cut carrots into match sticks; chop celery; press garlic; and slice onions and mushrooms. Set each aside individually.
3. Spray nonstick pan with cooking spray, place over medium heat and cook pork until juices run clear.
4. Spray second pan with cooking spray, place over medium heat and add remaining ingredients, except for sweet-and-sour sauce and green onion. Simmer for 10 minutes.
5. Combine veggie mixture with pork and pour over rice on plate.
6. Top with ½ tablespoon sweet-and-sour sauce and garnish with minced green onion.

Serves 6
Calories: 253
Fat: 6.4g
Carbohydrates: 21.5g
Protein: 25g

Internationally Inspired

Mexican Lasagna

Prep time: 10 minutes
Cook time: 20 minutes

Ingredients

1 c. onion

1 green pepper

1 lb. ground round

1 c. mild salsa

1-oz. packet taco seasoning

1 c. ATHENOS nonfat Greek yogurt

4½-oz. can diced green chilies

2 chipotle peppers in adobo sauce

16-oz. can BUSH'S® Refried Beans – Fat Free BUSH'S BEST

Nonstick cooking spray

4 low-carb whole wheat tortillas

1 c. salad greens

1 c. reduced-fat Mexican cheese

Serves 8
Calories: 279
Fat: 7.8g
Carbohydrates: 23g
Protein: 31g

1. Preheat oven to 350 degrees.
2. Dice onion and green pepper and add to ground round in skillet over medium heat. Cook until meat is browned.
3. Drain juices from meat and pour into bowl.
4. Mix salsa and taco seasoning into meat.
5. Whisk together yogurt, green chilies, diced chipotle peppers (with seeds removed) and refried beans.
6. Spray nonstick cooking spray on 9" x 13" baking pan and lay 2 tortillas along the bottom of the pan.
7. Spread meat mixture over tortillas and top with remaining 2 tortillas.
8. Spread yogurt-bean mixture over tortillas and bake uncovered for 20 minutes.
9. Top with salad greens, cheese, salsa and a dollop of yogurt before serving.

Caribbean Jerk Chicken

Prep time: 5 minutes
   plus 3 hours marinating time
Cook time: 10 minutes

Ingredients

1T. fresh thyme	½ T. Splenda
1 t. fresh sage	¼ c. low-sodium
2 cloves garlic	soy sauce
¼ c. onion	¾ c. white vinegar
1 Serrano chili pepper	¼ c. orange juice
¾ t. allspice	Juice of 1 lime
1 t. cayenne pepper	16 oz. chicken breast
½ t. nutmeg	Salt and pepper
½ t. cinnamon	

Serves 4
Calories: 144
Fat: 1.5g
Carbohydrates: 4g
Protein: 27.5g

1. Prepare ingredients: Chop thyme and sage, press garlic, and dice onion and chili pepper, removing seeds from pepper.

2. Combine all ingredients, except for chicken, salt and pepper, to create marinade.

3. Pour marinade over chicken breast and refrigerate for at least 3 hours.

4. Spray nonstick pan with cooking spray, place over medium heat and cook chicken and marinade together until chicken juices run clear.

5. Season with salt and pepper.

Mexican Frittata

Prep time: 10 to 15 minutes
Cook time: 30 to 45 minutes

Ingredients

15-oz. can BUSH'S® Black Beans
2 chipotle peppers in adobo sauce
15-oz. can diced tomatoes
4 c. egg whites
1 c. low-fat shredded mozzarella cheese
4 c. fresh spinach
Red pepper flakes
Salt and pepper
Nonstick cooking spray

1. Preheat oven to 350 degrees.

2. Prepare ingredients: Drain and rinse beans; dice peppers; drain tomatoes; and chop spinach into bite-sized pieces.

3. Combine eggs with all other ingredients, reserving ½ cup black beans.

4. Spray nonstick cooking spray on 9" square glass pan.

5. Press reserved ½ cup black beans into bottom of pan and pour the egg mixture over the bean crust layer.

6. Bake uncovered in oven for 30 to 45 minutes or until the center of the frittata is set.

Serves 4
Calories: 287.1
Fat: 5.7g
Carbohydrates: 20.5g
Protein: 35.3g

Curry Shrimp

Prep time: 5 minutes
Cook time: 15 minutes

Ingredients

¼ c. onion

1 clove garlic

2 T. fresh cilantro

½ T. olive oil

1 lb. shrimp, tail on

1 T. curry powder

⅓ c. ATHENOS nonfat Greek yogurt

Salt and pepper

1. Prepare ingredients: Chop onion and cilantro and press garlic. Set each aside individually.

2. Sauté garlic and onions in olive oil over medium heat until tender. Season with salt and pepper.

3. Add shrimp and curry powder to the pan and heat through. Season again with salt and pepper.

4. Stir in yogurt and cilantro.

5. Remove from heat and serve.

Serves 4
Calories: 143
Fat: 3g
Carbohydrates: 1.6g
Protein: 26g

Bruschetta

Prep time: 10 minutes
Cook time: 10 minutes

Ingredients

1 whole wheat baguette
½ c. canned tomatoes
3 oz. ATHENOS nonfat feta cheese
½ c. ATHENOS nonfat Greek yogurt
⅛ t. fresh oregano
⅛ t. fresh basil
¼ t. onion powder
Salt and pepper
1 Roma tomato

1. Preheat oven to 350 degrees.

2. Prepare ingredients: Slice bread into thin pieces; drain tomatoes; and chop oregano and basil.

3. Lay bread slices on baking sheet and bake for 5 minutes.

4. Stir together tomatoes, spices, feta and yogurt.

5. Spread tomato mixture onto bread.

6. Bake another 5 minutes.

6. Season with salt and pepper and garnish with fresh tomato slices and herbs.

Serves 6 (3 slices each)
Calories: 73
Fat: 2.5g
Carbohydrates: 6.6g
Protein: 6.7g

Shana says...

From curry powder to chili paste and sauerkraut to beans, international foods are wonderful to enjoy while on vacation or in the comfort of your own home. Many of these foods, however, also are high in calories and fat due to the method of preparation and are typically viewed as a "no-no" when living a healthy lifestyle. In this internationally inspired chapter, though, you will find no deep-fried items, which will leave you saying "yes-yes."

Enjoy the creaminess of curry made with Athenos nonfat Greek yogurt and spices, rather than the traditional recipe that is made with heavy creams that are high in fat and calories.

Let your mouth water when Asian dishes lighten up with limited amounts of oil and nuts, but still pack bold, intense flavors.

Mexican food with limited cheese and no sour cream will leave you feeling satisfied – you can count on it.

Jerk chicken will rock your taste buds! And, you'll see an interesting and very health-conscious take on your typical bruschetta.

So go ahead, have friends over. Entertain with Greek Kabobs, Sauerkraut Salad and Beef Bul Go Gi.

Taste all the flavors you love from a few different places—all with my own personal spin.

Enjoy!

Greek Kabobs

Prep time: 5 minutes plus 3 hours marinating
Cook time: 5 minutes

Ingredients

½ T. fresh thyme

³/₈ t. fresh oregano

4 cloves garlic

1 T. onion, chopped

½ c. English cucumber

2 T. lemon juice

½ c. chicken broth

1 lb. pork loin chop

1 c. ATHENOS nonfat Greek yogurt

Salt and pepper

1. Prepare ingredients: Chop thyme and oregano; press garlic; dice onion and cucumber; and remove the fat from pork loin and cut into small chunks. Set each aside individually.

2. Combine lemon juice, chicken broth, thyme, ¼ teaspoon oregano and ½ teaspoon garlic to create marinade sauce.

3. Place pork chunks in dish, pour sauce over top and marinate while covered for at least 3 hours in the refrigerator.

Serves 6
Calories: 180
Fat: 6g
Carbohydrates: 2g
Protein: 27.3g

4. Whisk together yogurt, cucumber, 1 tablespoon garlic, ⅛ teaspoon oregano, salt and pepper to create dip. Chill.

5. Skewer pork chunks on sticks and grill until juices run clear.

6. Season with salt and pepper and enjoy with cucumber dip.

Sauerkraut Salad

Prep time: 5 minutes
Cook time: No cooking required

Ingredients

½ c. canned or cooked beets

¼ c. red onion.

2 cloves garlic

1 c. sauerkraut

½ t. olive oil

1 t. balsamic vinegar

Salt and pepper

Serves 2
Calories: 51
Fat: 1g
Carbohydrates: 9g
Protein: 1.6g

1. Prepare ingredients: Cut beets into strips; slice onions into similar-sized strips; and press garlic.

2. Layer sauerkraut, beets, onion and garlic on a plate.

3. Drizzle with olive oil and vinegar.

4. Season with salt and pepper to taste.

Beef Bul Go Gi

Prep time: 5 minutes
   plus 3 hours marinating
Cook time: 20 minutes

Ingredients

1 lb. eye of round beef steak

2 T. water

2 T. no-calorie sweetener

2½ T. low-sodium soy sauce

2 T. sesame oil

2 cloves garlic

1 T. chili sauce

1 c. mushrooms

1 c. broccoli

½ c. onions

½ c. carrots

1. Cut eye of round into strips.

2. Combine water, no-calorie sweetener, soy sauce, sesame oil, pressed garlic and chili sauce to create marinade sauce.

3. Place beef strips in dish, pour sauce over top and marinate while covered for at least 3 hours in the refrigerator.

4. Prepare ingredients: Slice mushrooms and onions, and chop broccoli and carrots into bite-sized pieces.

5. Spray nonstick pan with cooking spray, place over medium heat and cook prepared veggies, beef strips and marinade until desired wellness.

6. Serve over cooked rice, if desired.

Serves 4
Calories: 222
Fat: 8.4g
Carbohydrates: 6.5g
Protein: 29g

Sweet Thang

Mixed Berry Protein Smoothie

Prep time: Less than 5 minutes
Blend time: 5 minutes

Ingredients

6 oz. low-calorie vanilla yogurt

1 scoop berry or cookies-and-cream protein powder
(21g – 23g protein; less than 3g carbs)

½ c. skim milk

½ c. water

½ c. frozen berries

No-calorie sweetener (optional)

1. Place all ingredients together in blender.

2. Blend until smooth and creamy.

3. Add no-calorie sweetener, if desired.

_____

Serves 1
Calories: 299.5
Fat: 0.5g
Carbohydrates: 34.9g
Protein: 33.3g
_____

Peanut Butter-Chocolate Cookies

Prep time: 5 minutes
Cook time: 10 minutes

Ingredients

½ c. high-protein,
    low-calorie organic cereal

½ c. honey creamy
    natural peanut butter

¼ c. no-calorie sweetener

1 egg white

½ scoop chocolate
    protein powder (21g – 23g
    protein; less than 3g carbs)

Serves 10
(2 cookies each)
Calories: 124
Fat: 6.6g
Carbohydrates: 8g
Protein: 5.5g

1. Preheat oven to 350 degrees.

2. Crush cereal.

3. Combine all ingredients in bowl and then form into 20 small dough balls.

4. Bake for 10 minutes, or until cookie is golden brown.

Sweet Thang

Peanut Butter-Banana Bundles

Prep time: 5 to 10 minutes
Cook time: 15 to 18 minutes

Ingredients

1 pkg. crescent roll dough

3 T. natural peanut butter

1 banana

24 semi-sweet chocolate chips

½ T. ground cinnamon

1 T. no-calorie sweetener

1. Roll out crescent dough, pinching perforations together to create one large sheet.

2. Cut dough into 12 equal squares.

3. Dollop ½ teaspoon of peanut butter onto center of each dough square.

4. Cut banana into 12 equal slices and place one slice on top of the peanut butter on each square.

5. Place 2 chocolate chips on top of each banana slice.

6. Bring corners of dough square to the center, over the top of the chocolate chips, and pinch to seal. Repeat for each square.

7. Dust bundle tops with cinnamon-sweetener mixture.

8. Bake 15 to 18 minutes, or until golden brown.

Serves 12
Calories: 130
Fat: 7.5g
Carbohydrates: 12g
Protein: 4g

English Muffin French Toast

Prep time: Less than 5 minutes
Cook time: 5 to 10 minutes

Ingredients

½ c. egg whites

1 t. vanilla extract

2 t. ground cinnamon

English muffin

Nonstick cooking spray

1 T. sugar-free raspberry preserves

2 T. low-sugar vanilla yogurt

1. Whisk together egg whites, vanilla and 1 teaspoon cinnamon. Set aside other teaspoon cinnamon for sauce.

2. Soak English muffin in egg mixture until spongy.

3. Spray nonstick pan with cooking spray and grill muffin until golden brown on each side.

4. Stir together preserves and yogurt until well-blended and spread over English muffin, stacking each half and layering sauce between.

Serves 1
Calories: 289.5
Fat: 8.3g
Carbohydrates: 38.1g
Protein: 18.2g

Sweet Thang

Pecan, Raspberry & Ricotta French Toast

Prep time: 5 minutes
Cook time: 10 minutes

Ingredients

2 thin slices pecan raisin bread

¼ c. liquid egg substitute

Nonstick cooking spray

½ c. fat-free ricotta cheese

1 T. low-sugar raspberry preserves

1 T. no-calorie sweetener

¼ c. whole fresh raspberries

1. Soak bread pieces in egg substitute, allowing bread to absorb most of egg.

Serves 1
Calories: 265.5
Fat: 2.2g
Carbohydrates: 44.8g
Protein: 21g

---

2. Spray nonstick skillet with cooking spray and cook bread until golden brown on each side. Remove from heat and place on plate.

3. Mix ricotta cheese, raspberry preserves and no-calorie sweetener in a bowl.

4. Spread half of ricotta-raspberry mixture on one slice of French toast, top with other slice of toast and cover top of second slice with remaining ricotta-raspberry mixture.

5. Garnish with whole fresh raspberries.

Fruit, Yogurt & Granola Parfait

Prep time: 5 minutes
Cook time: No cooking required

Ingredients

1 scoop cookies-and-cream protein powder (21g – 23g protein; less than 3g carbs)

4 oz. low-sugar vanilla yogurt

¹/₃ c. low-sugar/low-fat granola

¹/₃ c. fresh mixed berries

1. Blend together yogurt and protein powder until smooth.

2. Place layer of fresh berries in bottom of parfait glass.

3. Follow with layer of yogurt and then a layer of granola.

4. Repeat layers until parfait is complete.

_____

Serves 1
Calories: 328.2
Fat: 4.3g
Carbohydrates: 46.9g
Protein: 27.8g

_____

Sweet Thang

Cinnamon Banana Wrap With Honey Peanut Butter

Prep time: Less than 5 minutes
Cook time: No cooking required

Ingredients

2 T. low-calorie cinnamon yogurt

1 T. natural honey peanut butter

1 low-carb whole wheat wrap

½ banana

Sprinkle of cinnamon

1. Spread yogurt and peanut butter on center of whole wheat wrap.

2. Slice banana and place on top of yogurt-peanut butter layer.

3. Roll wrap up and sprinkle with cinnamon.

Serves 1
Calories: 258 • Fat: 11g
Carbohydrates: 32g • Protein: 12g

Cranberry-Raisin Stuffed Apples

Prep time: Less than 5 minutes
Cook time: 35 minutes

Ingredients

2 Gala apples

¼ c. dried cranberries

¼ c. raisins

½ T. plus 1 t. no-calorie sweetener

1 T. light maple syrup

2 sheets low-fat cinnamon graham crackers

1 t. butter, room temperature

½ t. fruit-flavored, sugar-free applesauce

Sprinkle of cinnamon

Serves 4
Calories: 115
Fat: 1.5g
Carbohydrates: 26g
Protein: 1g

1. Preheat oven to 350 degrees.

2. Cut apples in half and remove cores.

3. Stir together cranberries, raisins, ½ tablespoon sweetener and maple syrup.

4. Divide cranberry-raisin mixture equally and stuff centers of apples.

5. Place apples in glass dish and bake for 30 minutes.

6. Crush graham crackers until they become fine crumbs.

7. Combine cracker crumbs, remaining no-calorie sweetener, butter and applesauce, and sprinkle crumb mixture evenly over apples.

8. Bake 5 more minutes, remove from oven and sprinkle with cinnamon.

Cream Cheese Fruit Dip

Prep time: Less than 5 minutes
Cook time: 5 to 10 minutes

Ingredients

½ T. fresh mint

4 T. low-fat cream cheese

6 oz. low-fat vanilla yogurt

2 c. whole strawberries

2 c. melon

1. Chop fresh mint into fine pieces and set aside.

2. Cut melon into small chunks and set aside.

3. Blend together cream cheese, yogurt and mint until smooth and creamy.

4. Sprinkle mint on top of dip and serve with whole fruit and chunked melons or your choice of fresh fruit.

Serves 4
(with ½ c. whole strawberries
and ½ c. chunked melon)
Calories: 112
Fat: 3g
Carbohydrates: 18.6g
Protein: 4g

Chocolate Shake

Prep time: 5 minutes
Cook time: No cooking required

Ingredients

½ c. sugar-free,
    fat-free ice cream

1 scoop chocolate
    protein powder (21g – 23g
    protein; less than 3g carbs)

1 T. sugar-free
    raspberry preserves

Serves 1
Calories: 107.5
Fat: 4.3g
Carbohydrates: 16.2g
Protein: 25.8g

1. Combine all ingredients in a blender.

2. Blend until smooth, adding a small amount of water, if needed.

LC = Low-Carb
GF = Gluten-Free
V = Vegetarian
SS = Shana's Suggestions